TOEFL® MAP

MAP New TOEFL® Edition

Writing

Advanced

DARAKWON

TOEFL® MAP New TOEFL® Edition
Writing Advanced

Publisher Chung Kyudo
Editor Cho Sangik
Authors Jonathan S. McClelland, Shane Spivey
Proofreader Michael A. Putlack
Designers Park Narae, Park Bohee, Chung Kyuok

First published in March 2023
By Darakwon, Inc.
Darakwon Bldg., 211, Munbal-ro, Paju-si, Gyeonggi-do 10881
Republic of Korea
Tel: 82-2-736-2031 (Ext. 250)
Fax: 82-2-732-2037

Price ₩19,000
ISBN 978-89-277-8037-3 14740
        978-89-277-8025-0 14740 (set)

www.darakwon.co.kr

Photo Credits
Shutterstock.com

Components Main Book / Scripts and Answer Key
7 6 5 4 3 2 1   23 24 25 26 27

Introduction

Studying for the TOEFL® iBT is no easy task and is not one that is to be undertaken lightly. It requires a great deal of effort as well as dedication on the part of the student. It is our hope that by using *TOEFL® Map Writing Advanced* as either a textbook or a study guide, the task of studying for the TOEFL® iBT will become somewhat easier for the student and less of a burden.

Students who wish to excel on the TOEFL® iBT must attain a solid grasp of the four important skills in the English language: reading, listening, speaking, and writing. The Darakwon *TOEFL® Map* series covers all four of these skills in separate books across three different levels. This book, *TOEFL® Map Writing Advanced*, covers the writing aspect of the test at the advanced level. Students who want to read passages, listen to lectures, learn vocabulary words, and write essays in response to tasks that appear on the TOEFL® iBT will have their wishes granted by using this book.

TOEFL® Map Writing Advanced has been designed for use in both a classroom setting and as a study guide for individual learners. For this reason, it offers a comprehensive overview of the TOEFL® iBT Writing section. In Part A, the Integrated and Independent Tasks of the TOEFL® iBT Writing section are explained, and writing tips to assist students are included. In Part B, learners have the opportunity to build their background knowledge by studying reading passages, lectures, and writing tasks that have appeared on the TOEFL® iBT. In addition, each chapter includes vocabulary sections that enable learners to understand the words that frequently appear in the TOEFL® iBT Writing section and to incorporate them into their writing. Every chapter also features critical thinking questions to help learners become more adept at analyzing arguments made in the reading passages and lectures. Finally, in Part C, students can take 2 complete TOEFL® iBT practice tests. Each of these tests includes Integrated and Independent Writing Tasks that have appeared on the actual TOEFL® iBT Writing section. When combined, all of these practice exercises help learners prepare themselves to take and, more importantly, excel on the TOEFL® iBT.

TOEFL® Map Writing Advanced has a vast amount of information and should prove to be invaluable as a study guide for learners who are preparing for the TOEFL® iBT. However, while this book is comprehensive, it is up to each person to do the actual work. In order for *TOEFL® Map Writing Advanced* to be of any use, the individual learner must dedicate himself or herself to studying the information found within its pages. While we have strived to make this book as user friendly and as full of crucial information as possible, ultimately, it is up to each person to make the best of the material in the book. We wish you luck in your study of both English and the TOEFL® iBT, and we hope that you are able to use *TOEFL® Map Writing Advanced* to improve your skills in both of them.

Jonathan S. McClelland
Shane Spivey

TABLE OF CONTENTS

How Is This Book Unique?   6
How to Use This Book   8

Part A | Understanding Writing Question Types

Introduction 01   Writing Section   14
Introduction 02   Integrated Writing   16
Introduction 03   Independent Writing   25

Part B | Building Knowledge & Skills for the Writing Test

Chapter 01

Integrated Writing   Education: Football Stadiums   34
Independent Writing   Job Satisfaction vs. High Salary   42

Chapter 02

Integrated Writing   Political Science: The Monroe Doctrine   50
Independent Writing   Broad Knowledge vs. Specialized Knowledge   58

Chapter 03

Integrated Writing   Engineering: The Tacoma Narrows Bridge   66
Independent Writing   Making Decisions   74

Chapter 04

Integrated Writing   Environmental Science: Land Reclamation   82
Independent Writing   Leisure Time   90

Chapter 05

Integrated Writing   Literature: People Read Less Literature Today   98
Independent Writing   Keeping Up with World Events   106

Chapter 06

Integrated Writing Environmental Studies: Green Consumerism 114
Independent Writing Spending Money on International Issues 122

Chapter 07

Integrated Writing Business: Maintaining U.S. Policies Abroad 130
Independent Writing Class Attendance Should Not Be Required 138

Chapter 08

Integrated Writing Computer Science: Are Internet Encyclopedias Better? 146
Independent Writing Documentaries and Books 154

Chapter 09

Integrated Writing Archaeology: Is the Sphinx Actually Ancient? 162
Independent Writing Reading a Book a Second Time Is More Interesting 170

Chapter 10

Integrated Writing Chemistry: The Problems Caused by Sulfur Dioxide 178
Independent Writing Higher Education Is Only for Good Students 186

Chapter 11

Integrated Writing Zoology: The Purpose of Zebra Stripes 194
Independent Writing Art Galleries and Musical Performances vs. Sports Facilities 202

Chapter 12

Integrated Writing Psychology: TV Addiction 210
Independent Writing Traveling Is Better with a Tour Guide 218

Part C | **Experiencing the TOEFL iBT Actual Tests**

Actual Test 01 226
Actual Test 02 234

How Is This Book Different?

TOEFL® Map Writing Advanced is not a typical TOEFL® study book. Of course it is similar to other TOEFL® books in that it replicates the types of passages and questions test takers will encounter on the test. However, this book differs in its focus: critical thinking. *TOEFL® Map Writing Advanced* will teach test takers how to critically analyze the material they will see on the actual writing section of the TOEFL®, thereby giving them the skills needed to earn a top score on the test. Here are the standout features of this book:

Critical Thinking Questions

One of the most important features of *TOEFL® Map Writing Advanced* is the critical-thinking questions. These questions come after the reading passage and the lecture in each chapter. The questions after the reading passage ask students to make predictions about the contents of the lecture while the questions after the writing task ask them to examine the relationship between the arguments presented in the lecture and the reading passage.

Strong Responses Analysis

One of the best ways to learn is from examples. It is for this reason that each chapter includes a benchmark sample response after the student writing task. These benchmark responses let students see what makes a response strong and also allow them to deconstruct the answer to see how it presents the material from the reading passage and the lecture.

Weak Response Analysis

In addition to the benchmark responses in each chapter, *TOEFL® Map Writing Advanced* includes weak responses for students to analyze. The weak responses allow students to see common errors made by test takers and give them the opportunity to correct these mistakes. By doing this, students will learn what mistakes they should avoid in their own writing, thus increasing their chances for success on the actual TOEFL® iBT.

Rubric Mastery

Complementing the weak response analysis is the rubric mastery section. This section requires students to critically analyze weak responses and to assign a final grade utilizing a scoring rubric similar to the one used by the TOEFL® test graders. By understanding how essays are graded on the actual TOEFL® iBT, students will learn how to strengthen their responses in all of the key grading areas. The scoring rubrics appear in Part A of this book.

Tandem Note-Taking for Integrated Writing

While *TOEFL® Map Writing Advanced* includes the standard outlining sections after the reading passage and the lecture, it also includes a unique tandem note-taking section. The tandem note-taking section requires students to complete side-by-side outlines for both the reading passage and the lecture. Having notes for both the reading and the lecture next to each other on the same page will allow students to analyze the relationship between them more quickly, easily, and accurately.

Idea Boxes for Independent Writing

For many students, generating supporting ideas is the most difficult aspect of the Independent Writing Task. Therefore, this book includes idea boxes with sentences that will help them generate supporting ideas and examples for their essays.

Vocabulary Boxes

To earn a high score on the TOEFL® iBT, a strong vocabulary is essential. For this reason, each chapter in *TOEFL® Map Writing Advanced* includes three vocabulary boxes: two in the Integrated Writing Section and one in the Independent Writing Section. Each vocabulary box includes six to ten words and gives the part of speech, definition, and use in context for each word. This will enable students not only to recognize these words when they appear on the actual TOEFL® iBT but also to utilize them to make their writing more vivid and succinct.

How to Use
This Book

TOEFL® Map Writing Advanced is designed for use either as a textbook in a classroom in a TOEFL® iBT preparation course or as a study guide for individuals who are studying for the TOEFL® iBT on their own. *TOEFL® Map Writing Advanced* has been divided into three sections: Part A, Part B, and Part C. All three sections offer information that is important to learners preparing for the TOEFL® iBT. Part A is divided into 3 chapters that introduce the Writing section, the Integrated Writing Task, and the Independent Writing Task. Part B is divided into 12 chapters, each including passages and questions that have appeared on the TOEFL® iBT. Part C has 2 actual tests consisting of Integrated and Independent Writing Tasks that resemble those appearing on the TOEFL® iBT.

Part A Understanding Writing Question Types

This section is designed to acquaint learners with the TOEFL® iBT Writing section and is divided into 3 chapters. The first chapter provides an overview of the Writing section and explains the general requirements of the Integrated and Independent Writing Tasks. It also features an explanation on how to organize essays and includes an exercise for learners to complete. The second chapter breaks down the Integrated Writing Task by providing a detailed explanation of the question types and writing requirements. It also includes a sample Integrated Writing reading passage, a lecture, and a question. This chapter also provides writing tips, explains note-taking and the sample response sections included throughout the book, and includes learner exercises for both chapters. The final chapter breaks down the Independent Writing Task, providing a detailed explanation of the question types and writing requirements for this task. This chapter includes writing tips, emphasizes developing organizational skills when writing, and contains a sample Independent Writing Task question.

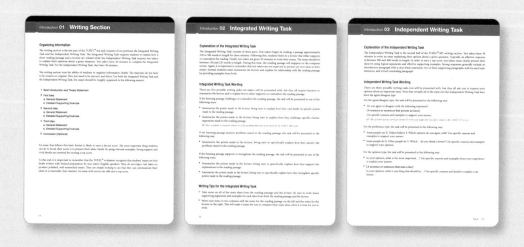

Part B Building Knowledge & Skills for the Writing Test

The purpose of this section is to introduce the various passages and topics that have appeared on the TOEFL® iBT. There are 12 chapters in Part B. Each one includes an Integrated Writing Task and an Independent Writing Task as well as vocabulary words and critical-thinking and sample response analysis exercises. Each chapter is divided into several parts.

Integrated Writing Task

Reading Passage

This section begins by introducing 6 to 10 new vocabulary words that appear in the reading passage. Along the right side of the reading passage are margins for note-taking, which allow students to get into the habit of taking notes as they read. Following the reading passage are note-taking and critical-thinking exercises designed to help students understand the reading passage and anticipate arguments that will be made in the lecture.

Lecture

This section is similar to the reading passage section. It introduces 6 to 10 new vocabulary words that are included in the lecture and features note-taking and critical-thinking exercises. In this section, the critical-thinking exercises are designed to help students analyze the relationship between the lecture and the reading passage, which will enable them to write a more accurate response for the writing task.

Tandem Note-Taking and Scaffolding

This section requires learners to write their notes from the previous two sections in two vertical columns. This arrangement allows students to expand their notes by adding supporting details from the reading passage and the lecture while allowing them to better understand the relationship between the two passages. At the end of this section is the scaffolding portion, which includes useful phrases for the students to incorporate into their responses.

Writing Section

This section includes the question for the Integrated Writing Task and provides space for learners to write their responses. It also features a writing guide to help students organize their essay as they write.

Strong Response

This section features a well-written response to the writing task given in the previous section. Students can see how to improve their own response by analyzing the organizational techniques, transitions, and vocabulary used in the strong response.

Weak Response

This section features a weak response that scores between 1 and 4 on the Integrated Writing Scoring Rubric. Students can see common mistakes to avoid while grading the essay according to the official Integrated Writing Scoring Rubric. At the end of this section is a critical-thinking exercise that allows learners to further analyze the potential strengths and weaknesses of the response.

Independent Writing Task

Generating Ideas

This section begins by presenting the Independent Writing Task question for the chapter. This is followed by an idea-generating exercise that assists students in developing supporting ideas for their response.

Planning and Scaffolding

This section consists of a detailed note-taking exercise that requires students to write their thesis statement, supporting ideas, and examples. At the end of this section is the scaffolding portion, which includes useful phrases for students to incorporate into their essay.

Writing Section

This section reintroduces the writing task for the chapter and provides space for students to write their responses. It also features a writing guide to help students organize their essay as they write.

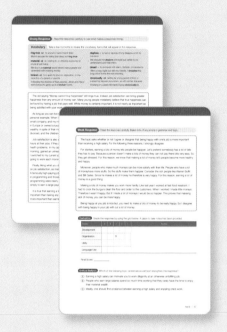

Strong Response

This section features a well-written response to the writing task given in the previous section and introduces 6 to 10 useful new vocabulary words. Students can see how to improve their own response by analyzing the organization, transitions, main ideas, and examples used in the strong response.

Weak Response

This section features a weak response that scores between 1 and 4 on the Integrated Writing Scoring Rubric. Students can see common mistakes to avoid while grading the essay according to the Independent Writing Scoring Rubric. At the end of this section is a critical-thinking exercise that allows students to further analyze the potential strengths and weaknesses of the response.

Part C Experiencing the TOEFL iBT Actual Tests

This section contains 2 complete TOEFL® iBT Writing section tests. The purpose of this section is to let students experience the actual Writing section and to see if they can apply the skills they have learned in the course of studying *TOEFL® Map Writing Advanced*.

Part

A

Understanding Writing Question Types

◊ **Introduction 01** Writing Section
◊ **Introduction 02** Integrated Writing Task
◊ **Introduction 03** Independent Writing Task

Organizing Information

The writing section is the last part of the TOEFL® test and consists of two portions: the Integrated Writing Task and the Independent Writing Task. The Integrated Writing Task requires students to explain how a short reading passage and a lecture are related while the Independent Writing Task requires test takers to explain their opinions about a given situation. Test takers have 20 minutes to complete the Integrated Writing Task. For the Independent Writing Task, they have 30 minutes.

The writing section tests the ability of students to organize information clearly. The responses do not have to be creative or original. They just need to be succinct and direct. For both the Integrated Writing Task and the Independent Writing Task, the essays should be roughly organized in the following manner:

1 Brief Introduction and Thesis Statement

2 First Idea
a. General Statement
b. Detailed Supporting Example

3 Second Idea
a. General Statement
b. Detailed Supporting Example

4 Third Idea
a. General Statement
b. Detailed Supporting Example

5 Conclusion (Optional)

An essay that follows this basic format is likely to earn a decent score. The most important thing students can do to boost their score is to present their ideas clearly by using relevant examples. Strong support and vivid details are essential for earning a top score.

To this end, it is important to remember that the TOEFL® evaluators recognize that students' essays are first drafts written with limited preparation by non-native English speakers. They do not expect test takers to produce polished, well-researched essays. They are simply looking to see that they can communicate their ideas in a reasonably clear manner. An essay with errors can still earn a top score.

Information Organization Exercise

Each of the following boxes contains ideas for an essay. Organize the information so that it fits logically into the outlines provided below.

Exercise 1

- Uniforms are not as expensive as brand-name clothing.
- Uniforms make it easy to get ready for school.
- School colors make students feel like they are a part of a group.
- One uniform costs little money.
- Uniforms create a sense of unity among students.
- Students do not have to waste time choosing clothing.
- Uniforms are a good idea.

1 Thesis Statement:

2 First Supporting Argument:

   Detailed Supporting Example:

3 Second Supporting Argument:

   Detailed Supporting Example:

4 Third Supporting Argument:

   Detailed Supporting Example:

Exercise 2

- Our solar system is shaped like a disk.
- Solid elements joined together in areas of high gravity.
- The sun retains ninety-nine percent of the cloud's mass.
- The planets formed in these areas.
- The nebular hypothesis states that our solar system was formed from a cloud of dust and gas.
- Most of the nebula's mass became the sun.
- Gravity caused the cloud to flatten and to become disk shaped.

1 Thesis Statement:

2 First Supporting Argument:

   Detailed Supporting Example:

3 Second Supporting Argument:

   Detailed Supporting Example:

4 Third Supporting Argument:

   Detailed Supporting Example:

Explanation of the Integrated Writing Task

The Integrated Writing Task consists of three parts. Test takers begin by reading a passage approximately 230 to 300 words in length for three minutes. Following this, students listen to a lecture that either supports or contradicts the reading. Finally, test takers are given 20 minutes to write their essays. The essays should be between 150 and 225 words in length. During this time, the reading passage will reappear on the computer screen. Again, it is important to remember that test takers are not expected to present any new ideas in their essays. Instead, students must summarize the lecture and explain its relationship with the reading passage by providing examples from both.

Integrated Writing Task Wording

There are five possible writing tasks test takers will be presented with, but they all require learners to summarize the lecture and to explain how it either supports or contradicts the reading passage.

If the listening passage challenges or contradicts the reading passage, the task will be presented in one of the following ways:

- Summarize the points made in the lecture, being sure to explain how they cast doubt on specific points made in the reading passage.
- Summarize the points made in the lecture, being sure to explain how they challenge specific claims/ arguments made in the reading passage.

  cf. *These questions account for almost all of the questions that have been asked on the TOEFL® iBT so far.*

If the listening passage answers problems raised in the reading passage, the task will be presented in the following way:

- Summarize the points made in the lecture, being sure to specifically explain how they answer the problems raised in the reading passage.

If the listening passage supports or strengthens the reading passage, the task will be presented in one of the following ways:

- Summarize the points made in the lecture, being sure to specifically explain how they support the explanations in the reading passage.
- Summarize the points made in the lecture, being sure to specifically explain how they strengthen specific points made in the reading passage.

Writing Tips for the Integrated Writing Task

- Take notes on all of the main ideas from the reading passage and the lecture. Be sure to write down supporting arguments and examples for each idea from both the reading passage and the lecture.
- Write your notes in two columns with the notes for the reading passage on the left and the notes for the lecture on the right. This will make it easier for you to compare their main ideas when it is time for you to write.

- Take one minute to organize your ideas before you begin writing. Refer to your notes as you write.

- Focus primarily on summarizing the lecture in your response. Be sure to include all of the main ideas and examples from the lecture. Do not give your opinion about the topic.

- Use only one or two sentences per paragraph to explain how the reading passage relates to the lecture.

- Begin each paragraph with clear, simple transitions.

- Manage your time wisely. Try to spend no more than five minutes writing each paragraph.

- Use the last one to three minutes to proofread your response. Make corrections as necessary.

Sample Integrated Writing Task

⊘ Reading Passage

On the Integrated Writing Task, a reading passage like the one below will be given to you first. You will have three minutes to read the passage.

Many public schools throughout the United States are facing enormous budget cuts and other financial and academic challenges. In this environment, many music education programs are in jeopardy. While supporters of music education are fighting desperately to keep it part of the required curriculum, it is best that music education be relegated to an extracurricular activity.

With student performance falling and academic standards rising, attracting talented and dedicated teachers should be the top priority for all schools across the nation. To do this, schools must be willing to pay teachers high salaries and to provide both teachers and students quality learning environments. For this to happen, schools must cut all programs that are not a part of standardized testing, namely music and art.

Proponents of music education often contend that music helps students perform better in subjects such as math and science. In reality, there is little concrete evidence to support these claims. On the contrary, while music is superficially rational, it is ultimately not a logical undertaking but rather is based primarily on intuition. To argue that music promotes logical thinking is itself irrational.

Finally, there is the discord between music education and our educational system. Our school system is predicated upon objectively grading student performance. With subjects that have definite answers, such as math and science, this is an easy proposition. However, music can never be graded objectively. By imposing a grading system upon music, schools are diminishing the true merit of music: to express oneself freely. Students who genuinely enjoy music do not need to be graded. If anything, grading will make music less appealing to them. Thus, music loses its value when it is incorporated into the mandatory curriculum.

Following this, you will listen to a lecture:

⊘ Lecture

Now listen to part of a lecture on the topic you just read about.

Professor (Female)

01-01

We hear a lot today about schools cutting their arts programs in order to compensate for slashed budgets. Many teachers and parents believe that students should focus on the three R's . . . and, um, maybe a little history and science for good measure. Unfortunately, by cutting art and music programs, schools may actually be preventing students from improving their academic performance.

Many argue that music programs are cost prohibitive. There is little justification for this. The reality is that sports programs are far more expensive to maintain than any music program. Schools often spend tens— if not hundreds of thousands of dollars—to build elaborate sports stadiums, to purchase team uniforms, and to pay coaches. Music programs, on the other hand, are um, not nearly as expensive . . . Most students buy and maintain their own instruments, and music teachers usually don't command six-figure salaries like most football coaches do.

Furthermore, recent studies have shown that learning how to play an instrument improves communication between the brainstem and the neocortex. By strengthening the relationship between these two areas of the brain, students, uh, develop higher brain functions that are used in math and science and also improve their listening comprehension and second language acquisition skills.

Another beneficial aspect of music education is that it has something Aristotle defined as extrinsic and intrinsic value. Let me elaborate. Music education has extrinsic value in that becoming a skilled musician can possibly lead to a fulfilling career in music as an adult. Of course, this is not true for every student. What is true for all students, though, is music's intrinsic value: the sheer joy it imparts on both the listeners and the musicians themselves. By studying music, students can become happier and more productive in other areas of their lives.

Once the listening is finished, the reading passage will reappear along with the following directions and the writing task:

⊘ Directions and Writing Task

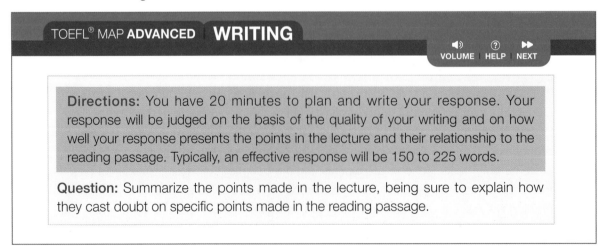

TOEFL® MAP ADVANCED **WRITING**

◀) VOLUME | ⑦ HELP | ▶▶ NEXT

Directions: You have 20 minutes to plan and write your response. Your response will be judged on the basis of the quality of your writing and on how well your response presents the points in the lecture and their relationship to the reading passage. Typically, an effective response will be 150 to 225 words.

Question: Summarize the points made in the lecture, being sure to explain how they cast doubt on specific points made in the reading passage.

At this time, you will have 20 minutes to complete your essay.

Note-Taking

To be successful on the writing portion of the TOEFL®, you must get into the habit of taking good notes. In order to do that, you must be able to identify the main ideas in a passage and differentiate them from supporting arguments and details.

⊘ Sample Notes

For the sample reading passage earlier in the unit, you should have written notes similar to the following:

1   Main Idea of the Passage: *Music education should not be included in the regular curriculum.*

2   First Supporting Argument: *Schools need to attract the best teachers possible.*

   need to offer teachers high salaries

   cut all programs not included in standardized testing

3   Second Supporting Argument: *Music education does not improve math and science ability.*

   little evidence to support this argument

   music does not rely on logic but rather intuition

4   Third Supporting Argument: *Music education does not fit well with our education system.*

   no definite answers; cannot be graded

   should not be graded; expression main pleasure

As you can see, these notes clearly summarize the main points of the reading while including the supporting details.

⊘ Note-Taking Exercise

You will now listen to the lecture. As you listen, complete the outline below. Try to make your notes as detailed as the ones given for the reading.

1   Main Idea of the Passage:

2   First Supporting Argument:

3   Second Supporting Argument:

4   Third Supporting Argument:

Tandem Note-Taking

Now that you have notes for both the reading and listening passages, it is time to fill in the tandem notes. These notes will help you when you write your response.

Reading	Listening
Main Idea	**Main Idea**
First Supporting Argument	**First Supporting Argument**
Supporting Detail	Supporting Detail
Second Supporting Argument	**Second Supporting Argument**
Supporting Detail	Supporting Detail
Third Supporting Argument	**Third Supporting Argument**
Supporting Detail	Supporting Detail

Writing Exercise

Use this page to write your response. You have 20 minutes to complete your essay.

▸ **First Paragraph**

State and discuss thesis

▸ **Second Paragraph**

First main idea from lecture

Supporting detail

Contradiction from reading

▸ **Third Paragraph**

Second main idea from lecture

Supporting detail

Contradiction from reading

▸ **Fourth Paragraph**

Third main idea from lecture

Supporting detail

Contradiction from reading

▸ **Fifth Paragraph**

Conclusion (optional)

Integrated Writing Scoring Rubric

Your response to the Integrated Task will be scored according to these criteria:

Score 5	A response scoring a 5 successfully summarizes the main ideas from the lecture and clearly explains how these arguments relate to those presented in the reading passage. Essays at this level are well organized and contain very few grammatical errors, which do not obscure the essay's meaning.
Score 4	A response scoring at this level is generally successful at presenting the main ideas from the lecture and explaining how they relate to those presented in the reading passage; however, it may have occasional lapses in clarity or accuracy. A response will also earn a score of 4 if it includes more frequent and noticeable grammatical errors that occasionally obscure meaning.
Score 3	A response scoring at this level explains some of the main ideas from the lecture and how they relate to those presented in the reading passage, but it does so in a way that is vague, unclear, or occasionally incorrect. A response that fails to include one of the main ideas from the lecture will also score at this level. Finally, essays scoring a 3 may also be characterized by more frequent grammatical errors that make it difficult to understand the relationship between the arguments made in the lecture and in the reading passage.
Score 2	A response scoring at this level includes only some of the important ideas from the lecture and fails to explain how they relate to the information presented in the reading passage. A response scoring a 2 may also include serious grammatical errors that prevent readers who are not already familiar with the topic from understanding the main ideas from the lecture and the reading passage.
Score 1	A response scoring at this level includes little or no useful information from the lecture. It may also include very low-level language that makes the essay incomprehensible.
Score 0	A response scoring at this level simply copies sentences from the reading passage, does not address the topic, is not written in English, or is blank.

Strong Response

Read the response carefully to see what makes a response strong. Place the following titles in the appropriate blanks in the response.

a. Contradictory sentence (×3)   b. Topic sentence (×3)   c. Thesis statement

d. Opening sentence   e. Example (×3)

[ ] The reading passage and the lecture both address the issue of music education in public schools. [ ] The lecture presents arguments in favor of maintaining music programs. Thus it goes against the central argument made in the reading passage.

[ ] First, the lecturer states that music programs are not cost prohibitive. The lecturer mentions that sports programs are far more expensive to maintain than music programs. [ ] The reasons are that music students pay for their own equipment and that music teachers are paid much lower salaries than most football coaches. [ ] These points contradict the reading passage's argument that music programs are too expensive to maintain.

[ ] Next, the lecturer argues that playing an instrument helps improve brain performance. [ ] The lecturer goes on to explain that by strengthening the relationship between parts of the brain, students enhance their math and science abilities while improving their listening skills and foreign language learning ability. [ ] This goes against the argument made in the reading passage that music does not help students perform better at other subjects.

[ ] The lecturer concludes by mentioning that music education has both extrinsic and intrinsic value. That is, it can lead to careers in music for some students while imparting a sense of joy in all music students. [ ] Because of this, the lecturer argues, students are able to become happier and more productive in other aspects of their lives. [ ] These arguments go a long way in rebutting the reading passage's claim that music education should not be incorporated into the educational system.

Weak Response

Read the response carefully. Make note of any errors in grammar and logic.

According to the lecture, the school must not cut there music programs because it does not help. Actually schools maybe hurting there performance by getting rid of music programs. The music program are not expensive, but the reading says music programs are a waist of money. The lecture says that school spend much more money to play football and salaries and music programs are not as expensive. So this means that schools must include music programs in their cirriculem.

Furthurmore, the lecture talks about playing music and making the connections inyour brain stronger. So student becomes better at math and sciences. The professor also say that playing a instrument makes your listening better and helps with second language learning.

Another reason that the lecture support music program is that music has a intrinsic and a extrinsic value which Aristotle said. The reading say music has no definite answers. So it should not be in school. However because music has a intrinsic and a extrinsic values, it is good to be in school.

⊘ Analysis Exercise

Grade the response by using the grid below. A place to take notes has been provided.

Score	5	4	3	2	1	Notes
Development						
Organization						
Unity						
Language Use			V			

Final Score: _____

Explanation of the Independent Writing Task

The Independent Writing Task is the second half of the TOEFL® iBT writing section. Test takers have 30 minutes to write an essay explaining their options about a given question. Typically, an effective response is between 300 and 400 words in length. In order to earn a top score, test takers must clearly present their ideas by using logical arguments and effective supporting examples. Strong responses generally include an introductory paragraph with a clear thesis statement, two or three supporting paragraphs with focused topic sentences, and a brief concluding paragraph.

Independent Writing Task Wording

There are three possible writing tasks you will be presented with, but they all ask you to express your opinion about an important issue. Note that virtually all of the topics for the Independent Writing Task have been the agree/disagree type.

For the agree/disagree type, the task will be presented in the following way:

- Do you agree or disagree with the following statement?

  [A sentence or sentences that present an issue]

  Use specific reasons and examples to support your answer.

  cf. This question type accounts for almost all of the essay topics that have been asked on the TOEFL® iBT so far.

For the preference type, the task will be presented in the following way:

- Some people say X. Others believe Y. Which opinion do you agree with? Use specific reasons and examples to support your answer.

- Some people do X. Other people do Y. Which… do you think is better? Use specific reasons and examples to support your opinion.

For the opinion type, the task will be presented in the following way:

- In your opinion, what is the most important…? Use specific reasons and examples from your experience to explain your answer.

- [A sentence or sentences that state a fact]

  In your opinion, what is one thing that should be…? Use specific reasons and details to explain your choice.

Writing Tips for the Independent Writing Task

- Take three to five minutes to brainstorm and to outline your response before you begin writing.
- Reword the question in your thesis statement.
- Make a few general statements about the topic in your opening paragraph.
- Include at least two main ideas in your essay to support your opinion.
- Illustrate your supporting ideas and examples from your personal experience and knowledge.
- Manage your time wisely. Try not to spend more than seven to ten minutes writing each paragraph.
- Use the last one to three minutes to proofread your response. Make corrections as necessary.

Sample Independent Writing Task

On the Independent Writing Task, you will be given the following directions along with a similar writing prompt:

⊘ Directions and Writing Task

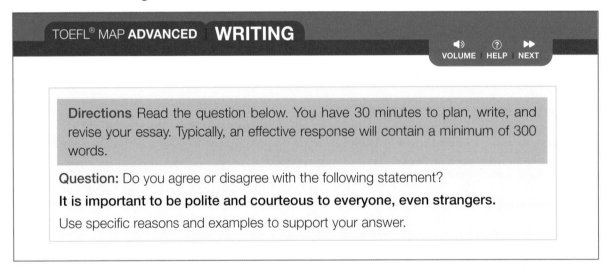

Generating Ideas

The following questions will help you write your response. Answer each with one or two sentences. Plan an answer for both options. Some ideas have been provided to help you.

> **⋆ Idea Box**
>
> **1** How can being polite make relationships with family and friends better?
> **2** How will people you do not know treat you if you are polite to them?
> **3** How can being polite to somebody affect that person's mood?

▷ **Agree**

Reason 1:

Reason 2:

Reason 3:

> **⋆ Idea Box**
>
> **1** Is it always possible to be polite? Explain.
> **2** How do you treat strangers differently from family and friends?
> **3** What are some times when it is better not to be polite?

▷ **Disagree**

Reason 1:

Reason 2:

Reason 3:

Outlining Exercise

To be successful on the writing portion of the TOEFL®, you must get into the habit of outlining your essay before you begin writing. Begin by writing your thesis statement and then arrange your supporting ideas logically. Finally, write down at least one supporting example for each supporting idea.

Planning

Use the outline to plan your response to the following: Do you agree or disagree with the following statement? It is important to be polite and courteous to everyone, even strangers. Use specific reasons and examples to support your answer.

Thesis Statement (Agree / Disagree) ....
....

First Supporting Idea ....
....

Supporting Example ....
....

Second Supporting Idea ....
....

Supporting Example ....
....

Third Supporting Idea ....
....

Supporting Example ....
....

Conclusion ....
....

Writing Exercise

Use this page to write your response. You have 30 minutes to complete your essay.

Do you agree or disagree with the following statement? It is important to be polite and courteous to everyone, even strangers. Use specific reasons and examples to support your answer.

▸ **First Paragraph**

State and discuss thesis

▸ **Second Paragraph**

First main supporting idea

Supporting detail

Example

▸ **Third Paragraph**

Second main supporting idea

Supporting detail

Example

▸ **Fourth Paragraph**

Third main supporting idea

Supporting detail

Example

▸ **Fifth Paragraph**

Conclusion

Independent Writing Scoring Rubric

Your response to the Independent Task will be scored according to these criteria:

Score 5	An essay scoring at this level effectively addresses the topic by utilizing logical organization, appropriate transitions between ideas and paragraphs, and developed supporting examples for each main idea. The essay will read smoothly and include a variety of sentence types, suitable word choice, and correct use of idiomatic expressions. It may also include minor grammatical errors that do not distract the reader.
Score 4	An essay scoring at this level generally addresses the topic well although it may not fully develop all supporting ideas. It is clearly organized for the most part, but it may include some unclear transitions, redundancies, and/or digressions. An essay at this level is fairly well developed, but it may lack sufficient detail to fully explain supporting ideas. It may also include more noticeable errors in grammar and word choice that do not obscure meaning.
Score 3	An essay scoring at this level addresses the topic using explanations and examples that are somewhat unclear and underdeveloped. It displays unity and coherence but may not include sufficient transitions between ideas. An essay scoring at this level may also include accurate but limited sentence structures and vocabulary and more frequent grammatical errors that occasionally obscure meaning.
Score 2	An essay scoring at this level fails to address the topic clearly and is characterized by inadequate organization and insufficiently developed ideas. It may include examples that fail to develop the main ideas and more numerous grammatical errors that obscure meaning.
Score 1	An essay scoring at this level fails to present and develop any ideas and includes serious and frequent grammatical errors that largely obscure meaning.
Score 0	A response scoring at this level simply copies the topic, does not address the topic, is not written in English, or is blank.

Strong Response

Read the response carefully to see what makes a response strong. Place the following titles in the appropriate blanks in the response.

a. Summary

d. Thesis statement

g. Final comment

b. Opening sentences

e. Example (×2)

c. General statement (×2)

f. Topic sentence (×2)

[ ] The world is becoming a ruder place. Children do not respect their elders. People do not hold doors open for others walking behind them. Customers use bad language when they do not get the service they want. [ ] In this world, where good manner and politeness are becoming increasingly scarce, I agree with the idea that it is important to be polite and courteous to everyone, even strangers.

[ ] Being polite to family members can directly impact your quality of life. [ ] You are around your family in your most private moments throughout your entire life. Therefore, you need to foster good relationships with your family members. [ ] Being rude to your family members simply because you have had a bad day at work does not facilitate harmony and can actually irritate them. But by using such basic courtesies such as "Please" and "Thank you" in the home, you can help members of your family grow closer to one another and help them feel relaxed and comfortable.

[ ] Being polite to strangers can both directly impact your life and indirectly impact all of society. [ ] Doing something as simple as holding a door open for a stranger can make that person feel less stressed while making yourself feel good. [ ] Indeed, research suggests that people living in polite societies tend to be happier. And by being courteous to others, you can influence them to be courteous as well. This will create a domino effect that will permeate throughout the whole of society, which will, in turn, improve the quality of life for everyone.

[ ] So the next time you decide against thanking your server at a restaurant, keep this thought in mind: Rudeness is a contagious disease. [ ] Instead of making the world a more hostile place by being rude, make it a more hospitable place by being courteous.

Weak Response

Read the response carefully. Make note of any errors in grammar and logic.

The topic says that being polite all the time is better. However I don't think that is the true.

Firstly, when you are all the time polite, people take advantage of you. Let me give example. When I was child, I was so polite. So then people weren't very nice to me. They think maybe I could not defence myself. Therefore, I changed to become less nice. What that happened I suddenly got more respect. This can be true for adults also. Say if you are bussness man. You have to deal people alot. If you are too nice, its like commit business suiside! Once you aren't so polite, those people will act more respect to you.

Secondly, most of the others people aren't too polite. So why should be polite at them? In other words, you shouldn't. When people aren't nice, you don't need to be polite, either. This mostly true with strager. Since you don't know them, can you take the benefits? I didn't think so. So I believe that treating others like you are being treated. In other word, when the other people are doing something to you, you are doing something likewise to them. For instance, if slam the door in your face when you walking, so do you too. But when people aren't too rude, then you can be not too rude back for them.

When you have politeness, sometimes its a good thing. But a lot of times, this is not true. The question said to be nice to others is more good then being rude. But like I said before it is better to not be polite with people most of time.

⊘ Analysis Exercise

Grade the response by using the grid below. A place to take notes has been provided.

Score	5	4	3	2	1	Notes
Development			V			
Organization						
Unity						
Language Use						

Final Score: _____

Building
Knowledge & Skills
for the Writing Test

Chapter 01

Integrated Writing
» Education: Football Stadiums

Independent Writing
» Job Satisfaction vs. High Salary

Education: Football Stadiums

Vocabulary Take a few moments to review the vocabulary items that will appear in this task.

pour *v* to move with a continuous flow
The rain **poured** down in sheets during the tropical storm.

gleaming *adj* something that shines with a steady light
The **gleaming** glass tower became the standout landmark in the city's skyline.

exorbitant *adj* excessive in quantity, size, or amount
Consumer rights groups protested the **exorbitant** prices charged by the electric company.

revenue *n* the total amount of income produced by a given source
Our company's annual **revenue** has decreased this year due to the global economic slowdown.

extracurricular *adj* not falling within the scope of the standard school curriculum
When I was in college, I participated in many **extracurricular** sports on campus.

tremendous *adj* unusually large; huge
My careless, wasteful spending has led to a **tremendous** amount of credit card debt.

topnotch *adj* of the highest quality; first rate
Our handcrafted shirts are made from only **topnotch** fabrics and materials.

garner *v* to collect; to accumulate
In an election, the winning candidate **garners** more votes than the losing candidate.

◈ **Reading** Read the passage carefully. Be sure to take notes in the margins about the main ideas and the supporting examples from each of the body paragraphs. You have 3 minutes to read.

In the past few years, high schools across the country have poured millions of dollars into their football programs. Some believe such spending is wasteful and even exorbitant. However, these schools are wholly justified in supporting their athletic teams as best they can for several reasons.

In many small communities, high school football is a major source of entertainment. In these places, football games bring in thousands of sports fans, and in order to attract more fans, schools must be willing to build clean and modern facilities. Consider the case of one high school that saw attendance at its football games nearly double after building a new five-million-dollar stadium. Thanks to its investment, the school was able to provide the community with a great source of entertainment in a clean and safe environment.

Another justification for schools to invest in their football teams is the potential increase in revenue. Schools that have invested in their football teams have been able to generate vast amounts of funding for various programs. For instance, one high school has been able to garner a fifty-thousand-dollar annual income from its football games, which it then used to pay for all of the other extracurricular programs at the school.

Perhaps the greatest benefit of high school football is that it provides troubled youths with a reason to stay in school. Schools that spend more money on their football programs are able to produce winning teams. And when a school has a winning team, more students are likely to try out. In

📖 **Margin Notes**

turn, this affords many young men a reason to stay in school, which has a tremendous impact on both individual students and the community at large. Therefore, it is only logical that schools spend the amount of money necessary to maintain topnotch football programs.

♦ **Note-Taking** Refer to the reading to complete the outline below.

1　Main Idea of the Passage: ....

....

2　First Supporting Argument: ....

....

3　Second Supporting Argument: ....

....

4　Third Supporting Argument: ....

....

Critical Thinking Consider the following questions. Answer them in complete sentences.

1　How does spending large amounts of money on football go against the mission of public schools?

2　How could the profits from a school's football program be used?

headline *n* the large-print words at the top of a newspaper story or article

Studies have shown that young people only read the **headlines** when they read the newspaper.

deal with *phr v* to handle or take care of a problem

The best way to **deal with** a bad situation in your life is to face it head on.

elaborate *adj* planned or executed with painstaking attention to detail

In spite of their **elaborate** escape plan, the bank robbers were still caught.

highlight *v* to bring attention to

In my speech today, I want to **highlight** the three most important issues that are damaging our company.

creed *n* a system of belief, principles, or opinions

The government has made laws preventing employers from discriminating based on a person's race or **creed**.

◊ **Listening**   Now listen to part of a lecture on the topic you just read about.

02-01

♦ **Note-Taking** Refer to the listening to complete the outline below.

1 Main Idea of the Lecture:

2 First Supporting Argument:

3 Second Supporting Argument:

4 Third Supporting Argument:

(Critical Thinking) Consider the following questions. Answer them in complete sentences.

1 In what ways does the professor refute the points made in the reading?

2 In what ways does the professor fail to address the arguments made in the reading?

◆ **Tandem Note-Taking** Refer to the outlines for the reading and the listening to complete the side-by-side notes below. Include only the three points from the reading and the listening that clearly contradict each other.

Reading

Main Idea

First Supporting Argument

Supporting Detail

Second Supporting Argument

Supporting Detail

Third Supporting Argument

Supporting Detail

Listening

Main Idea

First Supporting Argument

Supporting Detail

Second Supporting Argument

Supporting Detail

Third Supporting Argument

Supporting Detail

◈ Writing Use this page to write your response. You have 20 minutes to complete your essay.

Writing Guide	Summarize the points made in the lecture, being sure to explain how they cast doubt on specific points made in the reading passage.

▸ **First Paragraph**

State and discuss thesis

▸ **Second Paragraph**

First main idea from lecture

Supporting detail

Contradiction from reading

▸ **Third Paragraph**

Second main idea from lecture

Supporting detail

Contradiction from reading

▸ **Fourth Paragraph**

Third main idea from lecture

Supporting detail

Contradiction from reading

▸ **Fifth Paragraph**

Conclusion (optional)

The lecture completely refutes the reading passage. The professor's main purpose is to explain why school districts cannot afford to build elaborate football stadiums, and he does so by using three main supporting ideas.

He begins by mentioning the correlation between expensive football stadiums and spectator attendance. The reading suggests that building fancy stadiums increases attendance, but the listening contradicts this. The professor says that most football programs have not seen an increase in attendance for many years and that some have actually seen a decrease in attendance due to higher ticket prices.

The professor's next point is about funding. He illustrates this by referencing two schools that each spent twenty million dollars on football stadiums at a time when teachers are losing their benefits and textbook funding. Again, this goes against the reading, which mentions that high school football games "generate vast amounts of money" for schools.

The professor concludes his lecture by bringing up the purpose of public schools, which is to provide an equal education for all. While both the reading and the lecture agree that football programs can benefit the players, the lecture states that spending so much money just on football does not give all students the benefits they deserve.

Critical Analysis Refer to the sample response to complete the tasks below.

1 Underline the topic sentence in each paragraph.

2 Double underline the sentences that refer to the listening.

3 List some of the transitions the writer uses on the lines below.

_____

_____

Revising Use the guided sample response to help you revise your own response on the previous page. Be sure to incorporate specific vocabulary and phrasing from the guided sample response.

According to the lecture, the schools are spending so much money on football program. The professer gives three reason to support his arguement . His first argument is that schools maybe spending lots of money on football stadium but it doesn't help make games more fun to see. He says that schools have same attendance for many years and some schools have decreased attendance because tickets are too expensive. But the reading say that new stadiums causes more people to see the football games.

His second reason is schools are spending money when they can't afford to. He gives the example that Texas schools spend $20million on new football stadiums but they're not getting money to pay teachers and by books for their classes. Nevertheless, the reading say that schools make more money when they build elaborate football stadiums.

His third arguement is that school's do not keep in mind the purpose of public education which say that all students are treated equal. But he say spending lots of money on the football does not benefit all student. Only students who play the football. In this case, the reading say that having a good football team have tremendous impact on young men who would want to quit the school.

Evaluation Grade the response by using the grid below. A place to take notes has been provided.

Score	5	4	3	2	1	Notes
Development		V				
Organization						
Unity						
Language Use						

Final Score: _____

Critical Analysis Which of the following sentences could be added to help summarize the lecture?

- Ⓐ Studies have shown that schools benefit from investing in sports as well as academics.
- Ⓑ Additionally, a winning football team can benefit both the students and the community at large.
- Ⓒ He says that schools should spend money to attract talented teachers rather than to build elaborate football stadiums.

Job Satisfaction vs. High Salary

Q Do you agree or disagree with the following statement? Being happy with one's job is more important than receiving a high salary. Use specific reasons and examples to support your answer.

◊ **Generating Ideas** The following questions will help you write your response. Answer each with one or two sentences. Plan an answer for both options. Some ideas have been provided to help you.

> ☀ **Idea Box**
> **1** How does job satisfaction affect productivity?
> **2** What is the relationship between job satisfaction and stress?
> **3** What are the working conditions like at most high-salary jobs?

▷ **Agree**
Reason 1:

Reason 2:

Reason 3:

> ☀ **Idea Box**
> **1** What practical benefits does earning a high salary have?
> **2** In what ways can money bring happiness?
> **3** How can earning a high salary eventually lead to job satisfaction?

▷ **Disagree**
Reason 1:

Reason 2:

Reason 3:

◊ **Developing Ideas** Having examined the two options, which do you feel more comfortable developing into an essay?

◈ Planning Use the outline to plan your response to the following: Do you agree or disagree with the following statement? Being happy with one's job is more important than receiving a high salary. Use specific reasons and examples to support your answer.

Thesis Statement (Agree / Disagree)

First Supporting Idea

Supporting Example

Second Supporting Idea

Supporting Example

Third Supporting Idea

Supporting Example

Conclusion

Scaffolding Here are some useful phrases to help you when you write.

The old saying… still rings true.

I believe that happiness/a high salary is more important for…

While being happy at work/earning a high salary has its benefits, I feel that…

There are some things money cannot…

Happiness alone does not…

Having a lot of money can make a person…

Being happy at work can greatly boost…

Many high-paying jobs are…

To illustrate this…

Writing Guide	Do you agree or disagree with the following statement? Being happy with one's job is more important than receiving a high salary. Use specific reasons and examples to support your answer.

▸ **First Paragraph**

State and discuss thesis

▸ **Second Paragraph**

First main supporting idea

Supporting detail

Example

▸ **Third Paragraph**

Second main supporting idea

Supporting detail

Example

▸ **Fourth Paragraph**

Third main supporting idea

Supporting detail

Example

▸ **Fifth Paragraph**

Conclusion

Vocabulary Take a few moments to review the vocabulary items that will appear in this response.

ring true *exp* to sound or seem true or likely
Mark's excuse for being late does not **ring true**.

material *adj* of, relating to, or affecting economic or physical well-being
We live in a **material** world where many people are obsessed with making money.

broken *adj* torn apart by divorce, separation, or the desertion of a parent or parents
Following the divorce of their parents, Janet and Harry were forced to grow up in a **broken** home.

deplore *v* to feel or express strong disapproval of; to condemn
We should not **deplore** criminals but rather try to understand and help them.

dread *v* to anticipate with alarm, distaste, or reluctance
After a long night out with my friends, I **dreaded** the long drive home the next morning.

chronically *adv* lasting for a long period of time or marked by frequent recurrence, as with certain diseases
Working in a steel mill made Danny **chronically** ill.

The old saying "Money cannot buy happiness" still rings true. Indeed, job satisfaction can bring greater happiness than any amount of money can. Many young people mistakenly believe that true happiness can be found by having a job that pays well. While money is certainly important, it is not nearly as important as being satisfied with your work.

As long as you can live comfortably, money should not be an issue. To illustrate this, I will give a personal example. When I was growing up, my family was not rich. My father worked as a manager at a small company, and my mother worked as an elementary school teacher. Although we never vacationed in Europe or owned a luxury sedan, we were happy as a family. In contrast, our neighbors were quite wealthy. In spite of their material wealth, their family was not happy. Eventually, the husband and the wife divorced, and the children were left to grow up in a broken home.

Job satisfaction is also an important part of a healthy life. Most people spend at least half of their waking hours at their jobs. If they are not happy, they can suffer from depression, fatigue, stress, and many other health problems. In my case, I once worked at a high-paying job that I deplored. I dreaded waking up each morning, gained an unhealthy amount of weight, and became chronically fatigued. After only six months, I switched to my current job. Although I earn less than half as much money as I used to, I look forward to going to work each morning and now have enough energy to enjoy myself outside of work.

Finally, liking what you do is essential to working well. Job performance is almost entirely dependent on job satisfaction, as many studies have proven. One such study surveyed computer programmers. A famously high-paying job, computer programming attracts both people who are genuinely interested in programming and those who are in it only for the money. The study showed that those who enjoyed programming were nearly one hundred times more efficient coders that those who became programmers simply to earn a large paycheck.

It is true that earning a lot of money has its advantages. However, being happy with your life is more important than having any amount of money, and it is for this reason that being happy with your job is more important than earning a large paycheck.

Critical Analysis Refer to the sample response to complete the tasks below.

1 Underline the topic sentence in each paragraph.

2 Double underline the sentences that include supporting details.

3 List some of the examples the writer uses on the lines below.

_____

_____

Revising Use the guided sample response to help you revise your own response to the question. Be sure to incorporate specific vocabulary and phrasing from the guided sample response.

The topic asks whether or not I agree or disagree that being happy with one's job is more important than receiving a high salary. For the following three reasons, I strongly disagree.

For starters, earning a lots of money lets people be happyer. Let's pretend somebody has a lot of bills they has to pay. Because a person doesn't make a lots of money they can not pay there bills very easy. So they get stressed. For this reason, we know that making a lot of money let's people become more healthy and happy.

Moreover, people who make much moneys can be more satisfy with their life. People who have a lot of moneyhave more stuffs. So the stuffs make them happier. Consider the rich people like Warren Buffit and Bill Gates. Since he makes a lot of money he therefore is very happy. For this reason, earning a lot of money is a good thing.

Making a lots of money makes you work more hardly. Like last year I worked at fast food resatrant. I had to cook the burgurs clean the floor and order to the customers. When I worked I made little moneys. Therefore I wasn't happy. But if I made a lot of moneys I would be so happier. This proves that makeing alot of money, you can be more happy.

Being happy at you job is nice but, you need to make a lots of money to be really happy. So I disagree with being happy in your job with out a lot of money.

Evaluation Grade the response by using the grid below. A place to take notes has been provided.

Score	5	4	3	2	1	Notes
Development						
Organization			V			
Unity						
Language Use						

Final Score: _____

Critical Analysis Which of the following topic sentences would best strengthen this response?

- (A) Earning a high salary can motivate you to work diligently at an otherwise unfulfilling job.
- (B) People who earn large salaries spend so much time working that they rarely have the time to enjoy their material wealth.
- (C) Ideally, one should find a balance between earning a high salary and enjoying one's work.

Part

B

Chapter 02

Integrated Writing
◊ Political Science: The Monroe Doctrine

Independent Writing
◊ Broad Knowledge vs. Specialized Knowledge

Political Science: The Monroe Doctrine

Vocabulary Take a few moments to review the vocabulary items that will appear in this task.

foray *n* an initial attempt, especially outside of one's area

The action film star's **foray** into politics was surprisingly successful.

sovereignty *n* complete independence and self-government

The U.S. gained **sovereignty** from the U.K. following its victory in the Revolutionary War.

colonize *v* to move in and take control of an area

During the seventeenth and eighteenth centuries, the U.K. **colonized** many parts of the world.

retribution *n* the act of attacking in response to a first attack

I know I will face **retribution** for writing such a controversial book.

sphere *n* an area of power, control, or influence; a domain

During the nineteenth century, Britain's **sphere** of influence extended to every corner of the globe.

stem *v* to stop; to restrict

New laws have been introduced to **stem** the flow of illegal immigration.

amend *v* to make changes to a law; to correct; to fix

I really think you should try to **amend** your relationship with Kayla.

prohibit *v* to forbid by law or by an order

Smoking is **prohibited** in public restrooms.

intervene *v* to interfere, usually through force or threat of force, in the affairs of another nation

Any parties that **intervene** in the affairs of our nation will suffer serious consequences.

Reading Read the passage carefully. Be sure to take notes in the margins about the main ideas and the supporting examples from each of the body paragraphs. You have 3 minutes to read.

The Monroe Doctrine was one of the United States' first forays into international policy. Introduced on December 2, 1823, by President James Monroe, the doctrine stated that any efforts by European powers to colonize land or to interfere with states in the Americas would be viewed by the U.S. as acts of aggression requiring U.S. attention. In the 200 years since its introduction, the Monroe Doctrine has served as the cornerstone for maintaining the sovereignty of nations throughout the Americas.

Before the enactment of the doctrine, the U.S. had little influence beyond its shores. The doctrine changed this. It specified that no member of the Old World could attempt to colonize or otherwise affect nations located within the New World without facing retribution from the United States. Thus, the U.S. was able to extend greatly its sphere of influence throughout the Americas.

One of the main purposes of the doctrine was to stem the flow of colonization throughout the New World. President Monroe, after whom the doctrine was named, was morally opposed to colonization by European powers, and he stated, "The American continents, by the free and independent condition which they have assumed and maintain, are henceforth not to be considered as subjects for future colonization by

📖 **Margin Notes**

any European powers." The United States was able to provide former European colonies with the protection and the support they needed to gain sovereignty.

By preventing colonization, the doctrine promoted democracy and stability throughout the Americas. Changes made to the doctrine throughout the nineteenth century helped Central and South American nations become sovereign. One such example of this occurred in the 1870s, when President Ulysses S. Grant amended the doctrine to prohibit European powers from intervening in Latin American affairs.

◈ **Note-Taking** Refer to the reading to complete the outline below.

1　Main Idea of the Passage: ....

....

2　First Supporting Argument: ....

....

3　Second Supporting Argument: ....

....

4　Third Supporting Argument: ....

....

(Critical Thinking)　Consider the following questions. Answer them in complete sentences.

1　How did the U.S. benefit from keeping European powers out of the Americas?

2　Do you think the Monroe Doctrine ultimately helped other nations become independent?

Vocabulary Take a few moments to review the vocabulary items that will appear in this task.

superpower *n* a powerful and influential nation

The world's leading **superpowers** are the United States and China.

tacitly *adv* in an unspoken manner; implied

The lawmaker **tacitly** acknowledged the political risks of endorsing the unpopular plan.

yearn *v* to have a strong longing for; to covet

I **yearn** to return to my home country after being gone for nine years.

clout *n* influence; pull

As more women move into the workplace, they are gaining more **clout** in the office.

guise *n* a false appearance; a pretense

The thief was able to enter the apartment under the **guise** of being a police officer.

usurp *v* to seize and hold by force without legal authority

New York has recently **usurped** the title of the world's leading financial center from London.

double standard *n* a moral or ethical code that applies to one group more strongly than to another

Sandra complained that her father had a **double standard**; her younger brothers were allowed to date, but she was not.

check *v* to stop the motion of abruptly; to halt

Heavy rains **checked** the army's advance through the mountains.

hegemony *n* the predominant influence of one state over others

With the rise of China, the U.S.'s **hegemony** may be drawing to a close.

annex *v* to add territory to an existing nation

The city will determine whether or not to **annex** land east of Highway 75.

◊ Listening Now listen to part of a lecture on the topic you just read about.

02-02

◈ **Note-Taking** Refer to the listening to complete the outline below.

1 Main Idea of the Lecture: ....

....

2 First Supporting Argument: ....

....

3 Second Supporting Argument: ....

....

4 Third Supporting Argument: ....

....

(Critical Thinking) Consider the following questions. Answer them in complete sentences.

1 In what ways does the lecturer refute the points made in the reading?

2 In what ways does the lecturer fail to address the arguments made in the reading?

◆ Tandem Note-Taking
Refer to the outlines for the reading and the listening to complete the side-by-side notes below. Include only the three points from the reading and the listening that clearly contradict each other.

Reading

Main Idea

First Supporting Argument

Supporting Detail

Second Supporting Argument

Supporting Detail

Third Supporting Argument

Supporting Detail

Listening

Main Idea

First Supporting Argument

Supporting Detail

Second Supporting Argument

Supporting Detail

Third Supporting Argument

Supporting Detail

Scaffolding Here are some useful phrases to help you when you write.

The reading passage and the lecture mainly deal with...

The lecturer's arguments refute those made in the...

The reading suggests... but the listening completely contradicts this.

The professor then explains that...

She illustrates her point by referencing...

This directly rebuts the reading passage's claim that...

The lecturer concludes by mentioning...

◊ **Writing** Use this page to write your response. You have 20 minutes to complete your essay.

Writing Guide	Summarize the points made in the lecture, being sure to explain how they challenge specific claims made in the reading passage.

▸ **First Paragraph**

State and discuss thesis

▸ **Second Paragraph**

First main idea from lecture

Supporting detail

Contradiction from reading

▸ **Third Paragraph**

Second main idea from lecture

Supporting detail

Contradiction from reading

▸ **Fourth Paragraph**

Third main idea from lecture

Supporting detail

Contradiction from reading

▸ **Fifth Paragraph**

Conclusion (optional)

The lecturer talks about how the Monroe Doctrine was ultimately created to benefit the United States. Her arguments largely refute the points made in the reading passage.

The lecturer begins by agreeing with the reading's assertion that the U.S. was not a powerful nation when the doctrine was introduced. She says there is little evidence that the doctrine helped the U.S. gain any international authority and that it was created primarily to get the attention of Great Britain, which was the world's most powerful country at the time. This calls into question the reading passage's assertion that the doctrine helped the U.S. extend its sphere of influence.

The professor's next point is about the relationship between the doctrine and colonization. As the lecturer noted, the doctrine kept European powers out of the Americas, thereby allowing the U.S. to seize vast amounts of land from Spain and to carry out its goal of Manifest Destiny. This goes against the reading passage's claim that the doctrine prevented colonization.

Finally, the instructor argues that the doctrine was used to establish U.S. hegemony throughout the Americas. She illustrates this by mentioning how the U.S. relied on the doctrine to intervene on the conflict between Venezuela and Great Britain. Her argument rebuts the reading passage's argument that the U.S. created the doctrine to altruistically promote democracy.

Critical Analysis Refer to the sample response to complete the tasks below.

1 Underline the topic sentence in each paragraph.

2 Double underline the sentences that refer to the listening.

3 List some of the transitions the writer uses on the lines below.

_____

_____

Revising Use the guided sample response to help you revise your own response on the previous page. Be sure to incorporate specific vocabulary and phrasing from the guided sample response.

The reading and the lecture both talked about the Monroe Doctrine. The reading argues that the Monroe Doctrine created a better condition for the Latin America nation, which the professor disagreed with.

First of all, it was said that the Monroe Doctrine helps the US expands its influince to other nations. On the other hand, it was said that the Doctrine was more about crying for the attention. So perhaps it was not able to create more power for the US. In this way, the reading and professor were in opposition.

Next of all, the reading and listening again differs. It was mentioned that the document stem the flow of colonization around the New World, acoording to the President Monroe. This was contradiction by the fact that the US had it's many fest destiny, which made it go from both the coast.

Finally of all, the Doctrine helped keep the peace in the Americas. The President Ulysses made the Doctrine prohibit the European powers from influence Latin American affairs. This was unlike the argument made in the reading. There is was said that the Doctrine made a hay jemonie.

Evaluation Grade the response by using the grid below. A place to take notes has been provided.

Score	5	4	3	2	1	Notes
Development						
Organization		V				
Unity						
Language Use						

Final Score: _____

Critical Analysis Which of the following sentences could be added to strengthen the response?

Ⓐ President Ulysses S. Grant amended the doctrine so that European powers could not intervene in Latin American affairs.

Ⓑ Because of the doctrine, the U.S. was able to expand its territory.

Ⓒ According to the professor, the doctrine served to get the attention of Great Britain, which was the world's superpower at the time.

Broad Knowledge vs. Specialized Knowledge

 Q What is more beneficial, having a broad knowledge of various academic subjects or specializing in only one? Use specific reasons and examples to support your answer.

◈ **Generating Ideas** The following questions will help you write your response. Answer each with one or two sentences. Plan an answer for both options. Some ideas have been provided to help you.

☼ Idea Box

1 How does a broad knowledge base help with solving problems?
2 How can a generalized education help students figure out which subject they enjoy the most?
3 Do you think having a broad knowledge base makes it easier or more difficult to get a job?

▷ **Broad Knowledge**

Reason 1:

Reason 2:

Reason 3:

☼ Idea Box

1 How does specialized knowledge help with solving problems?
2 How does specialized knowledge make solving problems more difficult?
3 Do you think having specialized knowledge makes it easier or more difficult to get a job?

▷ **Specialized Knowledge**

Reason 1:

Reason 2:

Reason 3:

◈ **Developing Ideas** Having examined the two options, which do you feel more comfortable developing into an essay?

◈ Planning Use the outline to plan your response to the following: What is more beneficial, having a broad knowledge of various academic subjects or specializing in only one? Use specific reasons and examples to support your answer.

Thesis Statement (Broad Knowledge / Specialized Knowledge) ....

....

First Supporting Idea ....

....

Supporting Example ....

....

Second Supporting Idea ....

....

Supporting Example ....

....

Third Supporting Idea ....

....

Supporting Example ....

....

Conclusion ....

....

Scaffolding | Here are some useful phrases to help you when you write.

I believe that a broad/specialized education is…

While a broad/specialized education has its benefits, I feel that…

A broad education allows you to…

Mastery of one subject is more important than…

A broad education can teach you how to…

Individuals with specialized skills are able to… more easily.

To illustrate, I will share the experiences of…

In conclusion, I feel that a broad/specialized education is…

◈ Writing Use this page to write your response. You have 30 minutes to complete your essay.

Writing Guide	What is more beneficial, having a broad knowledge of various academic subjects or specializing in only one? Use specific reasons and examples to support your answer.

▸ **First Paragraph**

State and discuss thesis

▸ **Second Paragraph**

First main supporting idea

Supporting detail

Example

▸ **Third Paragraph**

Second main supporting idea

Supporting detail

Example

▸ **Fourth Paragraph**

Third main supporting idea

Supporting detail

Example

▸ **Fifth Paragraph**

Conclusion

Vocabulary Take a few moments to review the vocabulary items that will appear in this response.

revere *v* to regard with great awe and devotion
Many Americans **revere** great leaders from the past, such as George Washington and Abraham Lincoln.

polymath *n* a person of great or varied learning
Some of the most famous **polymaths** in history include Aristotle and Leonardo da Vinci.

jack-of-all-trades *n* a person who can do many different kinds of work
A **jack-of-all-trades** may be a skilled soccer player, accomplished musician, and talented carpenter.

preclude *v* to make impossible, as by action taken in advance; to prevent
To **preclude** the risk of injury, please make sure all items are properly stored in the overhead bins.

lucrative *adj* producing wealth; profitable
Buying real estate is nearly always a **lucrative** business venture.

self-worth *v* self-esteem; self-respect
Some argue that girls develop more **self-esteem** at single-sex schools.

Throughout history, many of the most successful and revered individuals were polymaths, those knowledgeable of numerous academic fields. But in today's increasingly fast-paced and technological society, a broad knowledge of various academic subjects is no longer useful. A specialized education is much more beneficial.

Specializing in one area allows you to master a subject. Fields such as pharmacology and accounting require the mastery of a deep set of skills. Anything less than complete understanding in these fields is unacceptable. The generalist, on the other hand, studies many fields but masters none, as in the saying, "Jack of all trades, master of none." A specialized education allows you to develop a level of mastery of a subject that a broad education precludes.

Individuals with specialized skills are able to land lucrative jobs more easily. Many of today's highest-paying jobs, such as engineer and computer programmer, require specialized knowledge. An engineer can only design and build a bridge by mastering specific kinds of mathematics and physics while a computer programmer must be proficient in several coding languages in order to write efficient, bug-free code. For high-salary jobs, a specialized education is essential.

Professionals with specialized knowledge tend to have a greater sense of purpose in life. To illustrate, I will share the experiences of two friends who recently graduated from university. One friend studied engineering; the other studied journalism. The journalism friend has not been able to find a steady job that he enjoys while the engineering friend recently started a high-paying career as a nuclear engineer. The journalism friend always complains about how meaningless his life is. The engineer friend simply enjoys his. For him, a specialized education has given him a greater sense of self-worth.

In the past, a generalized education was considered ideal. However, as illustrated above, this is no longer the case. For most people, obtaining a specialized education is much more beneficial as it can lead to a high-paying career and give a greater sense of purpose in life.

Refer to the sample response to complete the tasks below.

1 Underline the topic sentence in each paragraph.

2 Double underline the sentences that include supporting details.

3 List some of the examples the writer uses on the lines below.

_____

_____

Revising Use the guided sample response to help you revise your own response to the question. Be sure to incorporate specific vocabulary and phrasing from the guided sample response.

There are some people today who think a specialized education is essential. in many ways the are right. But if you consider the benefits of a generalized education you will see that its benefits outweigh its disadvantages.

For one, a generalized education cna help you find what you truely enjoy. If you only study one specialized subject, you will not know what an other subjects are like. An you may not learn, what you really enjoy. Take for example art. If you really like art but never study it how can you know? To learn about what you really like you need to study many different subjects.

The next thing, a generalized education helps you see things from many peoples points of view. Because you study many different subjects. If you study many different subjects you learn about how something can affect something else. Like a scientist who studies history can know that some kinds of experiments have very negative affects and have cuased problems in the past.

Finally if you study a generalized education, you will have more inerresting conversations. Since you know about many different subjects you can talk about many different things. One thing people think boring is some people who only know about one thing. If you learn a lot of different things you can discuss more interestingly. So for this reason, a generalized education has more benefit.

Evaluation Grade the response by using the grid below. A place to take notes has been provided.

Score	5	4	3	2	1	Notes
Development						
Organization						
Unity						
Language Use		V				

Final Score: _____

Critical Analysis Which of the following topic sentences would best strengthen this response?

Ⓐ A generalized education will make you a more adept critical thinker.

Ⓑ In our information-saturated society, the value of a generalized education is questionable.

Ⓒ Most ancient Greek philosophers had a generalized education.

Part
B

Chapter 03

Integrated Writing
◊ Engineering: The Tacoma Narrows Bridge

Independent Writing
◊ Making Decisions

Engineering: The Tacoma Narrows Bridge

Vocabulary   Take a few moments to review the vocabulary items that will appear in this task.

scant *adj* noticeably deficient in quantity, fullness, or extent

Given the high unemployment rate, there is a **scant** chance that Doug will find a new job.

aerodynamic *adj* related to the forces of wind against objects

A bus is less **aerodynamic** than a sports car.

contested *adj* in doubt or dispute

Seeing as the results of the study are **contested**, NASA is calling for a second round of testing.

buffet *v* to strike against forcefully; to batter

The storm waves **buffeted** the small craft caught out at sea during the typhoon.

rock *v* to sway violently, as from a blow or shock

The nation of El Salvador was recently **rocked** by powerful earthquakes.

span *n* the measure of space between two points or extremities, such as a bridge or roof

The **span** between the arches is eight feet.

self-perpetuating *adj* able to renew oneself or itself indefinitely

Poverty is a **self-perpetuating** problem, and it is therefore very difficult to prevent.

affix *v* to secure to something

The manager **affixed** the notice about employee terminations to the wall.

Reading   Read the passage carefully. Be sure to take notes in the margins about the main ideas and the supporting examples from each of the body paragraphs. You have 3 minutes to read.

📖 **Margin Notes**

The Tacoma Narrows Bridge was opened to traffic on July 1, 1940. A scant four months later, "Galloping Gertie" collapsed into the cold waters below. In the decades since its collapse, the bridge has become the prime example illustrating the importance of aerodynamics when constructing bridges. Although the exact causes of the bridge's failure remain contested, the theory of aerodynamic instability remains the most widely accepted.

One of the main factors contributing to the collapse was the narrowness of the bridge's main span. On the day of the collapse, the bridge was subjected to 42-mile-per-hour winds, which buffeted the main span of the bridge, causing it to rock violently. The exceptionally narrow main span of bridge began to twist in two opposite directions. This twisting motion became self-perpetuating and therefore prevented the bridge from returning to its rest position.

Further contributing to the twisting motion was the lack of support cables. The original design of the bridge called for support cables to be placed every six feet. But in order to reduce construction costs, the number of support cables was reduced by twenty-five percent, making the bridge less stable as a result. Had the bridge been built with the intended number of support cables, it most likely would have been able to resist the forces of the wind.

What ultimately could have prevented the collapse was the use of stronger construction materials for the bridge. Earlier suspension bridges, such as New York's Brooklyn Bridge, were constructed out of reinforced concrete trusses affixed to concrete piers. Such designs prevented these bridges from being affected by winds while allowing them to support heavier loads. The reliance on lightweight steel by the designers of the Tacoma Narrows Bridge ensured the bridge's fate.

Glossary **truss** *n* a rigid framework, as of wooden beams or metal bars, designed to support a structure, such as a roof

◈ **Note-Taking** Refer to the reading to complete the outline below.

1 Main Idea of the Passage: ....

....

2 First Supporting Argument: ....

....

3 Second Supporting Argument: ....

....

4 Third Supporting Argument: ....

....

(**Critical Thinking**) Consider the following questions. Answer them in complete sentences.

1 The main span of the Tacoma Narrows Bridge used solid steel plates that blocked the wind to support the roadbed. How do you think these may have contributed to the collapse?

2 Why do you feel the bridge designers did not use concrete in spite of its superior strength?

Vocabulary Take a few moments to review the vocabulary items that will appear in this task.

disputed *adj* contested; debated

The outcome of the big soccer match is being **disputed**, and some are calling for a rematch.

employ *v* to put to use; to utilize

The mayor plans to **employ** many different strategies to improve the city's reputation.

quadruple *v* to multiply or be multiplied by four

The colonel **quadrupled** the number of guards on base from four to sixteen.

vibration *n* shaking; quivering

The **vibrations** from my phone awoke me from my sleep.

slippage *n* movement away from an original or secure place

The financial crisis in Dubai has analysts worried about further market **slippage**.

insufficient *adj* not enough to meet a demand or requirement

One of the main reasons for the great number of casualties on the *Titanic* was the **insufficient** number of lifeboats.

reinforced *adj* strengthened; toughened

Reinforced concrete is much stronger than regular concrete.

shortsighted *adj* not carefully considering future consequences

The **shortsighted** plan failed to account for the city's future population growth.

◊ **Listening** Now listen to part of a lecture on the topic you just read about.

02-03

Glossary **self-excited** *adj* operating without an external source of power

◈ Note-Taking Refer to the listening to complete the outline below.

1 Main Idea of the Lecture: ....

....

2 First Supporting Argument: ....

....

3 Second Supporting Argument: ....

....

4 Third Supporting Argument: ....

....

(Critical Thinking) Consider the following questions. Answer them in complete sentences.

1 In what ways does the instructor refute the points made in the reading?

2 What examples does the instructor provide to support his argument?

♦Tandem Note-Taking Refer to the outlines for the reading and the listening to complete the side-by-side notes below. Include only the three points from the reading and the listening that clearly contradict each other.

Reading	Listening
Main Idea	**Main Idea**
First Supporting Argument	**First Supporting Argument**
Supporting Detail	Supporting Detail
Second Supporting Argument	**Second Supporting Argument**
Supporting Detail	Supporting Detail
Third Supporting Argument	**Third Supporting Argument**
Supporting Detail	Supporting Detail

◈ **Writing** Use this page to write your response. You have 20 minutes to complete your essay.

Writing Guide	Summarize the points made in the lecture, being sure to explain how they cast doubt on specific points made in the reading passage.

▸ **First Paragraph**

State and discuss thesis

▸ **Second Paragraph**

First main idea from lecture

Supporting detail

Contradiction from reading

▸ **Third Paragraph**

Second main idea from lecture

Supporting detail

Contradiction from reading

▸ **Fourth Paragraph**

Third main idea from lecture

Supporting detail

Contradiction from reading

▸ **Fifth Paragraph**

Conclusion (optional)

The reading passage and the lecture discuss the Tacoma Narrows Bridge collapse. The lecture posits that the bridge collapsed due to a flawed design, which runs contrary to the points made in the reading passage.

To begin with, the professor questions the reading's assessment that having a narrow main span contributed to the collapse of the Tacoma Narrows Bridge. He says that the width of the bridge could not affect the bridge's structural integrity in any way. Rather, it was the use of plate girders, which presented an obstacle for the wind, that contributed to the failure of the structure.

The professor then moves on to the issue of the lack of support cables. Though the reading says that a reduction in the number of support cables from the original design decreased the bridge's stability, the professor contends that there is little evidence to support this. He does admit that a lack of support cables may have contributed to the collapse, but he believes that the twisting was so severe that even doubling the number of support cables would not have prevented the collapse.

The professor concludes his lecture by discussing the bridge's building materials. While he concedes that the bridge would still be standing had it been built out of stronger materials, he says that a poor design was the ultimate determining factor. Had the bridge employed the more aerodynamic truss design, it would have remained standing to this day.

Critical Analysis ▷ Refer to the sample response to complete the tasks below.

1 Underline the topic sentence in each paragraph.

2 Double underline the sentences that refer to the listening.

3 List some of the transitions the writer uses on the lines below.

_____

_____

Revising ▷ Use the guided sample response to help you revise your own response on the previous page. Be sure to incorporate specific vocabulary and phrasing from the guided sample response.

The lecture that followed the reading passage about the Tacoma Narrows Bridge collapse, gave some doubt on the cause of the collapse.

Firstly, although the reading said the bridge collapsed because it was too narrow, the lectuere does not agree. He said that eventhough the bridge was quadrupled in wideness, it wouldn't have mattered because the bridge was built out of solid steel plates that were not aeordynamic.

Secondly, the reading says that not having enough support cables made the bridge callapse. However, the professor says that not enough cables was not problem, because the force of the road was too much for the cables to handle.

Thirdly, reading said if the bridge were made with stronger materials, it would still be standing, and the lecturer agreed. However, it suggests that stronger material would not help too much, and that use a truss design was more important. So it wasn't use of wrong materials that made the bridge callapse, but the wrong design.

Evaluation ▸ Grade the response by using the grid below. A place to take notes has been provided.

Score	5	4	3	2	1	Notes
Development						
Organization		V				
Unity						
Language Use						

Final Score: _____

Critical Analysis ▸ Which of the following sentences would best strengthen the response?

Ⓐ This design would have been much more aerodynamic and would have allowed wind to pass through the bridge much more easily.

Ⓑ The width of the main span played the most important role in the collapse of the bridge.

Ⓒ If the bridge had been constructed with the correct number of cables, it probably would not have collapsed.

Making Decisions

Q Do you agree or disagree with the following statement? A person should never make an important decision alone. Use reasons and examples to support your answer.

◈ **Generating Ideas** The following questions will help you write your response. Answer each with one or two sentences. Plan an answer for both options. Some ideas have been provided to help you.

> 💡 **Idea Box**
>
> **1** How can consulting others make it easier for your idea to become successful?
> **2** What are the benefits of having multiple opinions about a situation?
> **3** How can the advice of others make the decision-making process easier?

▷ **Agree**

Reason 1:

Reason 2:

Reason 3:

> 💡 **Idea Box**
>
> **1** How can asking for the advice of others make it more difficult to come to a decision?
> **2** Who is in the best position to determine your needs?
> **3** What might others think of you if you always ask them for advice?

▷ **Disagree**

Reason 1:

Reason 2:

Reason 3:

◈ **Developing Ideas** Having examined the two options, which do you feel more comfortable developing into an essay?

◊ Planning Use the outline to plan your response to the following: Do you agree or disagree with the following statement? A person should never make an important decision alone. Use reasons and examples to support your answer.

Thesis Statement (Agree / Disagree) ....

....

First Supporting Idea ....

....

Supporting Example ....

....

Second Supporting Idea ....

....

Supporting Example ....

....

Third Supporting Idea ....

....

Supporting Example ....

....

Conclusion ....

....

Writing Guide	Do you agree or disagree with the following statement? A person should never make an important decision alone. Use reasons and examples to support your answer.

▸ **First Paragraph**

State and discuss thesis

▸ **Second Paragraph**

First main supporting idea

Supporting detail

Example

▸ **Third Paragraph**

Second main supporting idea

Supporting detail

Example

▸ **Fourth Paragraph**

Third main supporting idea

Supporting detail

Example

▸ **Fifth Paragraph**

Conclusion

consult *v* to seek advice or information

I **consulted** with my parents before making my decision to marry Amy.

imperative *adj* urgent; pressing

It is **imperative** that you file your taxes immediately to avoid paying any fines.

counsel *n* advice or guidance, especially from a knowledgeable person

When faced with financial troubles, I sought **counsel** from my friends and family.

assess *v* to determine the value, significance, or extent of

Following the flood, the insurance team came to our home to **assess** the damage.

conundrum *n* a difficult problem; a dilemma

The war in the Middle East is the great **conundrum** facing lawmakers today.

mitigate *v* to moderate in force or intensity of; to alleviate

Following the car accident, I took several different medications to **mitigate** my pain.

endeavor *n* an attempt to achieve something

Our company has received the funding we needed to begin our **endeavor** to research new forms of energy.

Our lives are filled with major decisions. Switching careers. Buying a new car. Starting a business. Getting married. Decisions like these can have tremendous impact on our lives and the lives of those we love. Because of this, I believe it is essential to consult with others when making important decisions.

One of the strongest arguments in favor of consulting with others is the issue of impact. A major decision affects not only your life but also the lives of others. Let me explain with a personal example. I recently got married. This decision impacted not only my life but also the lives of my husband and our families. In this situation, I was not able to make my decision alone. Rather, I had to consult with the people who would be affected by the outcome of my decision to marry before I could make my decision.

Impact is not the sole justification for consulting with others, however; there is also the issue of gaining new perspectives. When you make an important decision, it is imperative to consider all available options. Oftentimes, you cannot do this alone, which is why it is essential to seek the counsel of others when making such decisions. Even high-ranking leaders, such as the president of the United States, seek the opinions of others before making decisions. By consulting with others, you are better able to assess all potential outcomes in order to make the best decision possible.

Finally, there is the issue of confidence. When you are faced with a difficult decision, you may not be certain that your solution will be well received. Unsure of yourself, you may fail to execute your plan successfully. This potential conundrum can be easily mitigated by consulting with, and therefore gaining approval from, others. For instance, I once considered changing my career, but I was not confident that it was a wise decision to do so. I therefore asked my friends and co-workers for advice. When they supported my endeavor, I gained the confidence I needed to execute my plan successfully.

To sum up, making the best decisions is an important part of living a happy life. For the reasons given above, it is imperative to get advice from others when making important decisions.

Critical Analysis Refer to the sample response to complete the tasks below.

1 Underline the topic sentence in each paragraph.

2 Double underline the sentences that include supporting details.

3 List some of the examples the writer uses on the lines below.

_____

_____

Revising Use the guided sample response to help you revise your own response to the question. Be sure to incorporate specific vocabulary and phrasing from the guided sample response.

The question says that people shouldnot make important decisions alone. However I disagree for 3 reasons.

the first raeson is that one you know what's best for you. That to say, others can not make your decision for you. For example, maybe you want to get a baby, but you ask others opinon. If they tell you not to get a baby, how do you know its right?Only you can chose, what's right.

Second reason is that making decisions alone means you choose quicker. If you ask many people for there opinon it takes alot of time. For instance there's a car you want but you have to take it soon. Since you ask the others opinon you can not, take the car. So you have to make a decision quickly, you should not, ask others opinons because it waists time.

The final reason is that decision making alone means you can only decion. To illustrate, if you ask others opinons you can not know whose to choose it is, nevertheless making decision alone means you know whose it fault. for these 3 reasons I think making decisions alone is best.

Evaluation Grade the response by using the grid below. A place to take notes has been provided.

Score	5	4	3	2	1	Notes
Development						
Organization						
Unity				V		
Language Use						

Final Score: _____

Critical Analysis Which of the following topic sentences would best strengthen this response?

If you had just made a decision without hesitating, you would have been able to get what you wanted.

Ⓐ Body paragraph 1

Ⓑ Body paragraph 2

Ⓒ Body paragraph 3

Part

B

Chapter 04

Integrated Writing
◊ Environmental Science: Land Reclamation

Independent Writing
◊ Leisure Time

Environmental Science: Land Reclamation

Vocabulary Take a few moments to review the vocabulary items that will appear in this task.

clay *n* a type of soil that is often used to make pottery
The soil in this area is mostly **clay** so is not particularly good for farming.

wetlands *n* land that has wet, spongy soil
Many birds, fish, and mammals live in the **wetlands** in the local region.

dike *n* an embankment that is built to hold back water or to control its flow
There are many **dikes** near the river to keep it from flooding the city.

residential *adj* relating to a home or homes
There are few factories and businesses located in **residential** areas.

border *v* to be next to
The two countries **border** each other for more than 500 kilometers.

artificial *adj* manmade; not natural
There are thousands of **artificial** satellites orbiting the Earth.

profitable *adj* creating a profit; making money
His investment in the company was highly **profitable**, so he retired at a young age.

cramped *adj* very limited in space; confined
The elevator had fifteen people in it, so they all felt **cramped**.

◆ **Reading** Read the passage carefully. Be sure to take notes in the margins about the main ideas and supporting examples from each of the body paragraphs. You have 3 minutes to read.

📖 **Margin Notes**

Land reclamation is the process through which new land is created from the sea. This can be done in a variety of ways. One is by filling a watery area with large rocks and concrete and then putting clay and dirt on top of it. Another is by draining wetlands such as swamps and marshes. Land reclamation provides a number of benefits.

The primary advantage is that it increases the amount of usable land in an area. For instance, a large part of the Netherlands is reclaimed land. This land was recovered from the sea through a complicated system of dikes and canals. Today, it is used as farmland and residential areas. Land reclamation has therefore provided more land for people in the Netherlands to develop, which has improved the economy of the country.

Another benefit is that reclaimed land almost always borders the ocean or the sea. In some cases, such as in Dubai, artificial islands are created from reclaimed land. Seafront property is typically more valuable than land farther inland. The reason is that many people want to build residences or businesses near water. This makes reclaiming land profitable for the companies and governments that engage in it.

Finally, as the global population increases, people need more places to live. Land reclamation helps provide these individuals with areas where they can have residences. For instance, some residential areas in Singapore are constructed on reclaimed land. This small nation has a population of millions and needs all the space it can find to house everyone. Without the use of reclaimed land, people would be even more cramped than they already are.

♦ **Note-Taking** Refer to the reading to complete the outline below.

1 Main Idea of the Passage: ....

....

2 First Supporting Argument: ....

....

3 Second Supporting Argument: ....

....

4 Third Supporting Argument: ....

....

(Critical Thinking) Consider the following questions. Answer them in complete sentences.

1 Do you think it is all right for people to reclaim land from the sea? Explain why you feel this way.

2 How is the argument about making artificial islands flawed?

Vocabulary — Take a few moments to review the vocabulary items that will appear in this task.

drain *v* to remove the water from

You need to **drain** the pool completely before you try to clean it.

bog *n* an area of land mostly containing wet, spongy ground with decaying plant material

Be careful in the **bog** because lots of venomous snakes live there.

storm surge *n* a rise in the sea level along the coast due to stormy weather

Because of the **storm surge**, water from the ocean traveled far inland and flooded many places.

marine *adj* relating to the sea

Marine animals such as sharks sometimes can be found in swamps near the ocean.

breeding ground *n* a place where animals go to mate and lay eggs or give birth to young

Ducks use this area of land as their **breeding ground** after they fly south for the winter.

displace *v* to cause someone or something to leave its home

Many people were **displaced** when the war between the two nations began.

tremendous *adj* great in number, amount, size, etc.

He lost a **tremendous** amount of money in the stock market.

◈ Listening — Now listen to part of a lecture on the topic you just read about.

02-04

◈ Note-Taking Refer to the listening to complete the outline below.

1 Main Idea of the Lecture: ....

....

2 First Supporting Argument: ....

....

3 Second Supporting Argument: ....

....

4 Third Supporting Argument: ....

....

(Critical Thinking) Consider the following questions. Answer them in complete sentences.

1 In what ways does the lecturer refute the points made in the reading?

2 What examples does the lecturer provide to support her arguments?

◈ **Tandem Note-Taking** Refer to the outlines for the reading and the listening to complete the side-by-side notes below. Include only the three points from the reading and the listening that clearly contradict each other.

Reading

Main Idea

....

....

First Supporting Argument

....

....

Supporting Detail

....

....

Second Supporting Argument

....

....

Supporting Detail

....

....

Third Supporting Argument

....

....

Supporting Detail

....

....

Listening

Main Idea

....

....

First Supporting Argument

....

....

Supporting Detail

....

....

Second Supporting Argument

....

....

Supporting Detail

....

....

Third Supporting Argument

....

....

Supporting Detail

....

....

◈ Writing Use this page to write your response. You have 20 minutes to complete your essay.

Writing Guide	Summarize the points made in the lecture, being sure to explain how they cast doubt on specific points made in the reading passage.

▸ **First Paragraph**

State and discuss thesis

▸ **Second Paragraph**

First main idea from lecture

Supporting detail

Contradiction from reading

▸ **Third Paragraph**

Second main idea from lecture

Supporting detail

Contradiction from reading

▸ **Fourth Paragraph**

Third main idea from lecture

Supporting detail

Contradiction from reading

▸ **Fifth Paragraph**

Conclusion (optional)

Both the lecture and the reading passage are about land reclamation. In her lecture, the professor casts doubt on the points made in the reading passage.

To begin, the professor notes that much reclaimed land used to be wetlands. She claims these areas, which include swamps and mangrove forests, are effective at preventing flooding as well as stopping storm surges. She believes flooding will be a problem in the future if some land is reclaimed. In this way, she goes against the argument in the reading passage that reclaimed land can improve a country's economy.

Next, the professor discusses how artificial islands are recovered from reclaimed land. While the reading passage states that these islands are valuable land since they border the sea, the professor does not think creating artificial islands is a good idea. She points out that many used to be coral reefs, which are important to marine ecosystems.

Last, the professor tells the class about the danger to local wildlife when land is reclaimed. She says some endangered birds live in an area which is going to be reclaimed. She argues that some species there may go extinct, too. In this way, she refutes the argument made in the reading passage, which states that reclaimed land provides extra space for the growing global population to live on.

Critical Analysis Refer to the sample response to complete the tasks below.

1 Underline the topic sentence in each paragraph.

2 Double underline the sentences that refer to the listening.

3 List some of the transitions the writer uses on the lines below.

_____

_____

Revising Use the guided sample response to help you revise your own response on the previous page. Be sure to incorporate specific vocabulary and phrasing from the guided sample response.

The reading passage think land reclaims is good. The professor doesn't like it. She wants no land to get the reclaimed.

She talks about the wetlands. She likes the wetlands. She says there are many swamps. The swamps stop storms. But the reading wants to get rid of the swamps. It wants to make farms and homes on reclaimed land.

Next are artificial islands. Both the reading and the professor like artificial islands. She thinks many fish and other animals will live near the islands. That is good.

The professor talks about endangered animals. She don't want animals to go extinct. She wants birds in the swamps. The reading wants more land for people. I think people are better than animals. I like the reading. I think the reading has the best ideas.

Evaluation Grade the response by using the grid below. A place to take notes has been provided.

Score	5	4	3	2	1	Notes
Development						
Organization						
Unity				V		
Language Use						

Final Score: _____

Critical Analysis Which of the following sentences would best strengthen the response?

(A) The professor opposes reclaiming land to make artificial islands since it would harm marine species.

(B) According to the professor, more endangered species live in wetlands than in any other ecosystem.

(C) The professor believes that making a profit is less important than preserving the environment.

Leisure Time

Q Do you agree or disagree with the following statement? People will have more leisure time in the future than they do today. Use reasons and examples to support your answer.

◆ **Generating Ideas** The following questions will help you write your response. Answer each with one or two sentences. Plan an answer for both options. Some ideas have been provided to help you.

> **Idea Box**
>
> **1** How can technology increase the amount of leisure time people have?
> **2** In what ways have work schedules changed over the past few decades?
> **3** Has leisure time become more important or less important to people over time?

▷ **Agree**

Reason 1:

Reason 2:

Reason 3:

> **Idea Box**
>
> **1** How can technology decrease the amount of leisure time that people have?
> **2** In many ways, people have become more competitive. How does this affect leisure time?
> **3** Explain how people's spending habits might reduce the amount of leisure time they have.

▷ **Disagree**

Reason 1:

Reason 2:

Reason 3:

◆ **Developing Ideas** Having examined the two options, which do you feel more comfortable developing into an essay?

◈**Planning** Use the outline to plan your response to the following: Do you agree or disagree with the following statement? People will have more leisure time in the future than they do today. Use reasons and examples to support your answer.

Thesis Statement (Agree / Disagree) ....

....

First Supporting Idea ....

....

Supporting Example ....

....

Second Supporting Idea ....

....

Supporting Example ....

....

Third Supporting Idea ....

....

Supporting Example ....

....

Conclusion ....

....

| Writing Guide | Do you agree or disagree with the following statement? People will have more leisure time in the future than they do today. Use reasons and examples to support your answer. |

▸ **First Paragraph**

State and discuss thesis

▸ **Second Paragraph**

First main supporting idea

Supporting detail

Example

▸ **Third Paragraph**

Second main supporting idea

Supporting detail

Example

▸ **Fourth Paragraph**

Third main supporting idea

Supporting detail

Example

▸ **Fifth Paragraph**

Conclusion

Vocabulary ⏐ Take a few moments to review the vocabulary items that will appear in this response.

scrape out *phr v* to achieve something with great difficulty

The young man from the countryside tried to **scrape out** a living in the big city.

meager *adj* lacking in fullness, quantity, or amount

My **meager** salary is not enough to support my growing family.

pronounced *adj* strongly marked; distinct

One of Jason's distinguishing features is his **pronounced** limp when he walks.

key *adj* of crucial importance; significant

One of the **key** factors to becoming rich is learning how to save money.

white-collar *adj* relating to workers who are usually college educated and work in offices

Accounting is a **white-collar** job while construction is a blue-collar job.

flexible *adj* responsive to change; adaptable

As a writer, my schedule is **flexible**: I work only when I want to.

tedious *adj* tiresome by reason of length, slowness, or dullness; boring

Working as a grocery store cashier is one of the most **tedious** jobs in the world.

undoubtedly *adv* without question; certainly

Angelina Jolie was **undoubtedly** once the most famous female actress in the world.

In the past, most people had very little leisure time. At that time, people had to work long hours in unsafe conditions to scrape out a meager living. Today, however, this is no longer the case. Changes in work culture and developments in technology have led to a greater value being placed on leisure time. These changes will only continue to become more pronounced as time passes. As a result, people will have more leisure time in the future than they do today.

One of the key developments leading to this increase in leisure time has been changes to work culture. In the past, many people worked twelve or more hours per day, seven days per week, doing difficult work such as coal mining or farming. Simply surviving was the main goal for most people. But over the course of the twentieth century, people become more educated and began working in offices and doing other white-collar jobs. Eventually, the now-traditional forty-hour workweek was established. Today, more and more people have task-based positions that give them greater flexibility in when, where, and how much they work. In the future, these types of jobs will become more common, thus leading to increased leisure time.

The main factor that has brought about such changes in the workplace is technology. Developments in technology, such as cell phones, the Internet, and even robotic tractors, have made older jobs more efficient while creating new jobs that are less tedious and time consuming. Consequently, people spend less time and work and more time relaxing. Furthermore, many of these same technological advancements have also made it possible for people to spend their free time more efficiently. No longer do people have to spend hours driving to their destination or riding on a slow-moving train. Technology such as the jetliner and the bullet train has made traveling more efficient and allow people to spend their free time as they should: relaxing. As this technology advances in the future, people will come to have even greater amounts of leisure time.

In the past, virtually no one had any leisure time. But thanks to changes in the workplace brought on by changes to work culture and developments in technology, people can now afford to spend most of their time relaxing. As the impact of these changes increases in the future, the amount of leisure time that people have will undoubtedly increase as well.

Critical Analysis Refer to the sample response to complete the tasks below.

1 Underline the topic sentence in each paragraph.

2 Double underline the sentences that include supporting details.

3 List some of the examples the writer uses on the lines below.

_____

_____

Revising Use the guided sample response to help you revise your own response to the question. Be sure to incorporate specific vocabulary and phrasing from the guided sample response.

Leisure time! Who doesn't want more leisure time? Although people have more leisure time now then they use to, it won't increase in the future. In other words, I do not agree that people will have more leisure time in the future for the following reasons.

Firstly, although technology has in some way made our lifes easier it has made our lives more difficult. Technology like the cell phone and the lap top keep us connected to our work. That is to say, we cannot ever escape from work. So, in actually, our leisure time is not leisure time it is just another work time. So therefore, eventhough people spend less hours in the office they are spending more hours working. As the technology improves and makes connectivity more commonplace, this fact will only become more true.

Secondly, because people have more expensive spending habits, they have to work harder to make more money. This is called keeping up with the Joneses. For instance, if you neighbor buys a luxury sedan, you have to buy a luxury sedan, too, in order to keep up with him. In order to do this, people have to work harder to make more money. Consequently, they have less leisure time. In the future, when more people become more wealthy, they will also want to keep up with the Joneses. What this mean is that as time passes people will spend more time working as less time having leisure.

Finally, in order to stay competitive and make lots of money, people will have to increase their credential and certification. In other words, people will take a lot of time to study in addition to working full time. So, people will work 40 hours per week and then they will spend a lot of time studying in order to get a better job. And even when the people get a better job, they will want to make more money, so they will continue to work a lot to keep up with the Joneses. What this means is that, even though people will have a lot of technology and a lot of money, they will not have much leisure time.

People today have much time for leisure. But in the future, like the reasons mentioned above, they will not have as much leisure time as they do today.

Evaluation Grade the response by using the grid below. A place to take notes has been provided.

Score	5	4	3	2	1	Notes
Development						
Organization	V					
Unity						
Language Use						

Final Score: _____

Critical Analysis In which of the following ways should the highlighted sentence be rewritten?

Ⓐ Second, research shows that in the future, people's spending will increase as their salary does.

Ⓑ Secondly, people will have to spend more time working to maintain their increasingly expensive spending habits.

Ⓒ Second of all, as people's spending habits increase, so do their salaries.

Chapter 05

Integrated Writing
◊ Literature: People Read Less Literature Today

Independent Writing
◊ Keeping Up with World Events

Literature: People Read Less Literature Today

Vocabulary Take a few moments to review the vocabulary items that will appear in this task.

run the gamut *exp* to cover a whole range
The viewers' reactions to the movie **ran the gamut** from delight to disgust.

sustain *v* to keep in existence; to maintain
The historical society works to **sustain** cultural treasures in our area.

insight *n* a deep, thorough, or mature understanding
A moment's **insight** is sometimes worth a life's experience.

atrophy *n* a wasting away or deterioration
Since leaving college, I have suffered from intellectual **atrophy**.

profound *adj* thorough; far reaching
Philosophers attempt to learn **profound** truths about the world.

bolster *v* to support; to reinforce
Playing with my children really **bolsters** my spirits when I am feeling blue.

instant gratification *exp* satisfaction gained from impulsive behavior
Video games are enjoyable because they offer **instant gratification**.

delve *v* to search deeply and laboriously
To prove her client's innocence, Sandra had to **delve** into the court's records.

engage *v* to attract and hold the attention of; to engross
Gardening is hobby that can **engage** you for hours at a time.

sustenance *n* a source of materials to nourish the body
I require a glass of orange juice and a tray full of fruit for my morning **sustenance**.

Reading Read the passage carefully. Be sure to take notes in the margins about the main ideas and supporting examples from each of the body paragraphs. You have 3 minutes to read.

In the past, reading literature was the primary source of entertainment for most people. Today, with all of the entertainment options in the world, which run the gamut from television to movies to music, it is no surprise that people read literature far less often than they used to. This change in the way people entertain themselves has had some profound effects on society.

The act of reading literature assists people in developing their imaginations. Great pieces of literature require readers to visualize for themselves the complex worlds contained within these works. In addition, many novels contain complex imagery and symbolism, making extensive use of metaphors to convey profound concepts. To grasp the meaning of literary works, readers must concentrate and analyze the words on the page. In doing so, they enhance their critical thinking and analytical skills while bolstering their imaginations.

Reading literature also develops and sustains culture. Literature acts as a cultural record, reflecting the nature of society and providing insight on the human condition. By reading literature, people come to better understand the essence of culture and human nature, which, in turn,

📖 **Margin Notes**

leads to the development of cultural traditions. The reason is that literary readers are much more likely to attend and participate in performing art events as well as visit art and history museums. In order to prevent cultural atrophy, it is clear that people must read literature.

Unfortunately, many people today choose the instant gratification found in movies and music. The decline in literary reading suggests a kind of mental laziness in which most people are unwilling to put forth the effort necessary to delve into a complex work of literature. While these modern forms of entertainment engage the mind to some extent, they are no substitute for the intellectual sustenance offered by a good book.

Glossary **imagery** *n* the use of vivid or figurative language to represent objects, actions, or ideas
symbolism *n* the use of symbols in literature to represent things such as ideas and emotions
metaphor *n* a figure of speech in which a word or phrase that ordinarily designates one thing is used to designate another, thus making an implicit comparison

◈ **Note-Taking** Refer to the reading to complete the outline below.

1 Main Idea of the Passage:

2 First Supporting Argument:

3 Second Supporting Argument:

4 Third Supporting Argument:

Critical Thinking Consider the following questions. Answer them in complete sentences.

1 What other forms of media can help develop culture?

2 Do you think only literature can develop the imagination? Explain why you feel this way.

Vocabulary Take a few moments to review the vocabulary items that will appear in this task.

lament *v* to express grief for or about; to mourn
The band members **lamented** the death of their lead singer.

genocide *n* the systematic destruction of an entire group or race
German Nazis committed **genocide** against the Jewish people.

horrific *adj* causing horror; terrifying
After seeing **horrific** sights on the battlefield, young Francis was unable to continue fighting.

tragic *adj* very sad
The unexpected death of the musical prodigy was **tragic**.

tabloid *n* a newspaper with many pictures and short articles that is printed on short sheets
Most **tabloids** publish sensational stories, like sightings of aliens and Elvis Presley.

multifaceted *adj* having many aspects, uses, or abilities
Most cell phones today are **multifaceted** devices able to perform dozens of different tasks.

multitude *adj* a very great number
A **multitude** of problems, including global warming and AIDS, face the world today.

abstruse *adj* difficult to understand
All of the texts were **abstruse** to Mike.

monotony *n* tedious; sameness or repetitiousness
I simply cannot stand the **monotony** of my daily routine.

◊ Listening Now listen to part of a lecture on the topic you just read about.

02-05

◈ **Note-Taking** Refer to the listening to complete the outline below.

1 Main Idea of the Lecture: ....

....

2 First Supporting Argument: ....

....

3 Second Supporting Argument: ....

....

4 Third Supporting Argument: ....

....

(**Critical Thinking**) Consider the following questions. Answer them in complete sentences.

1 In what ways does the instructor refute the points made in the reading?

2 In what ways does the instructor fail to address the arguments made in the reading?

◆**Tandem Note-Taking** Refer to the outlines for the reading and the listening to complete the side-by-side notes below. Include only the three points from the reading and the listening that clearly contradict each other.

Reading

Main Idea

....

....

First Supporting Argument

....

....

Supporting Detail

....

....

Second Supporting Argument

....

....

Supporting Detail

....

....

Third Supporting Argument

....

....

Supporting Detail

....

....

Listening

Main Idea

....

....

First Supporting Argument

....

....

Supporting Detail

....

....

Second Supporting Argument

....

....

Supporting Detail

....

....

Third Supporting Argument

....

....

Supporting Detail

....

....

Scaffolding Here are some useful phrases to help you when you write.

The lecturer discusses… and thus contradicts the reading passage's claim that…

The professor further asserts that…

She illustrates this by mentioning…

Another main point is that…

She argues this point by mentioning…

The professor's argument thus goes against the reading, which says…

This argument addresses the reading passage's assumption that…

◈ **Writing** Use this page to write your response. You have 20 minutes to complete your essay.

Writing Guide	Summarize the points made in the lecture, being sure to explain how they challenge specific claims made in the reading passage.

▸ **First Paragraph**

State and discuss thesis

▸ **Second Paragraph**

First main idea from lecture

Supporting detail

Contradiction from reading

▸ **Third Paragraph**

Second main idea from lecture

Supporting detail

Contradiction from reading

▸ **Fourth Paragraph**

Third main idea from lecture

Supporting detail

Contradiction from reading

▸ **Fifth Paragraph**

Conclusion (optional)

The lecturer discusses the effects of the decline of literary reading. She presents information that suggests the decline is not harmful and thus contradicts the reading passage's claim that the shift away from reading literature has negatively affected society.

First of all, the lecturer says that while people are not reading as much as they used to, the total number of people who read has risen. The professor goes on to explain that today's most popular books are deep, multifaceted texts. She further asserts that these texts are intellectually stimulating and engaging. This contradicts the reading passage's claim that only literature can provide intellectual stimulation.

Another main point is that many other forms of nonliterary activities, such as music and television, exist. The professor argues that these forms of media offer not only entertainment but also additional creative outlets. She further contends that the decrease in reading is the result of cultural changes and that these new forms of media develop culture in the same way novels do. The professor's argument thus goes against the reading, which says that only literature develops and sustains culture.

Finally, the professor explains that the decrease in literary reading may be caused by the books themselves. She explains that a majority of literary works are too difficult to be enjoyed and that a lot of people want a relaxing way to spend their free time. This argument addresses the reading passage's assumption that most people are too lazy to read literature.

Critical Analysis ▸ Refer to the sample response to complete the tasks below.

1 Underline the topic sentence in each paragraph.

2 Double underline the sentences that refer to the listening.

3 List some of the transitions the writer uses on the lines below.

_____

_____

Revising ▸ Use the guided sample response to help you revise your own response on the previous page. Be sure to incorporate specific vocabulary and phrasing from the guided sample response.

According to lecutre, the decline in literature is not a tradgedy that its made to be, people aren't reading literature too much these days, however they still read other books which are stimulating to the intellectual. Another fact is that these people are reading sciense and history books which have multy facits, considering this you cannot say, that people are too lazy to reading.

The lecutre also explense that the televins and the music also develpe culture like the novel does, because changes to technology make change to the culture. This unlike the reading beucase it say that only literature develop culture.

The other argument the professor she say that literaautre can not be enjoyed because people just want to relax. She say that people look for enterainment to ecape the monotany of life and that literature cannot do this.

Since this points are made, the listening and reading are in opposite, Becuae of this points the reading and listening the reader dobut if less reading litureaure is too bad, the professer explains that other books can still be good for the culture.

Evaluation Grade the response by using the grid below. A place to take notes has been provided.

Score	5	4	3	2	1	Notes
Development						
Organization			V			
Unity						
Language Use						

Final Score: _____

Critical Analysis Which of the following sentences would best strengthen the response?

Ⓐ This refutes the point made in the reading passage about the negative relationship between culture and changes in entertainment.

Ⓑ Although the reading passage suggests that there are fewer readers today, the professor says this is not the case.

Ⓒ Her statement goes against the reading passage's argument that literature alone reflects culture.

Keeping Up with World Events

 Q Do you agree or disagree with the following statement? It is important to keep up with world events even if they do not affect your life. Give reasons and examples to support your opinion.

◈ **Generating Ideas** The following questions will help you write your response. Answer each with one or two sentences. Plan an answer for both options. Some ideas have been provided to help you.

> 💡 **Idea Box**
>
> 1 By following news events from other places, how do you bolster your understanding of events in your area?
> 2 How can events in other countries indirectly affect your life?
> 3 From a humanitarian perspective, why should you follow world events?

▷ **Agree**

Reason 1:

Reason 2:

Reason 3:

> 💡 **Idea Box**
>
> 1 Why might people not be able to keep up with world events even if they want to?
> 2 To what extent can you understand the events occurring in a place with which you have no connection?
> 3 How can following world news stories negatively affect your emotions?

▷ **Disagree**

Reason 1:

Reason 2:

Reason 3:

◈ **Developing Ideas** Having examined the two options, which do you feel more comfortable developing into an essay?

◈Planning Use the outline to plan your response to the following: Do you agree or disagree with the following statement? It is important to keep up with world events even if they do not affect your life. Give reasons and examples to support your opinion.

Thesis Statement (Agree / Disagree) ....

....

First Supporting Idea ....

....

Supporting Example ....

....

Second Supporting Idea ....

....

Supporting Example ....

....

Third Supporting Idea ....

....

Supporting Example ....

....

Conclusion ....

....

Scaffolding Here are some useful phrases to help you when you write.

With a wealth of information readily available, the following question arises…

It is not as though these people do not care about…

Related to this is the issue of…

As the old saying goes…

Even if people… they would not be able to…

On the whole, it makes little sense to…

For the reasons given above, it is better to…

Writing Guide	Do you agree or disagree with the following statement? It is important to keep up with world events even if they do not affect your life. Give reasons and examples to support your opinion.

▶ **First Paragraph**

State and discuss thesis

▶ **Second Paragraph**

First main supporting idea

Supporting detail

Example

▶ **Third Paragraph**

Second main supporting idea

Supporting detail

Example

▶ **Fourth Paragraph**

Third main supporting idea

Supporting detail

Example

▶ **Fifth Paragraph**

Conclusion

Vocabulary   Take a few moments to review the vocabulary items that will appear in this response.

at one's fingertips *exp* to have something readily available to one

That police officer has the personal information of every citizen **at her fingertips**.

be consumed [with] *exp* to be affected very strongly by or to be obsessed with an idea

Michelle **is consumed with** making straight A's.

errand *n* a short trip to do something

My first **errand** today is to go to the bank to cash this check.

relevant *adj* having a connection with the matter at hand

Note that only **relevant** questions will receive a response.

stay abreast [of] *exp* to have the most recent information about something

Our monthly meetings allow everyone to **stay abreast of** recent developments at the company.

burden *n* a source of great worry or stress; a weight

The **burden** of the company's poor performance rests not on the executives but the workers.

taxing *adj* burdensome; wearing

I have a **taxing** work schedule this month.

pragmatically *adv* dealing or concerned with facts or actual occurrences; practical

Pragmatically speaking, you should wait to buy a new car until you get a new job.

fathom *v* to come to understand

I cannot **fathom** the meaning of the metaphors in the poem.

With a population of roughly eight billion, the world is filled with thousands, if not millions, of news events each day. With news stories from around the globe readily available at your fingertips, the following question arises: Is it important to keep up with world events even if they do not affect your life? For the following three reasons, I do not believe so.

For one, most people are consumed with the events in their own lives. On a typical day, most people have to do several errands, such as dropping their kids off at school, finishing a report before a meeting, having lunch with a new business client, or being on time for soccer practice. In short, most people are simply too busy to keep up with events that are in no way relevant to them. It is not as though these people do not care about what is happening elsewhere in the world. It is that they merely do not have enough time to stay abreast of these events.

Related to this is the issue of unnecessary emotional burdens. News stories are such because they are shocking, tragic, or horrific. In other words, most news stories are emotionally taxing. Considering the emotional burden brought about by watching the news, why should people follow these tragic stories from half a world away? Pragmatically speaking, they should not. Most people already have enough stress in their lives, and following news stories from around the world would only add to this emotional burden. As the old saying goes, ignorance is bliss.

Even if people were to follow news stories that do not affect them, they would not be able to understand the true nature of the events. Understanding the significance of events such as economic situations or political elections requires a profound knowledge of a country's history, culture, and language. Outsiders with no connection to the country simply cannot fathom these types of events. On the whole, considering how difficult it is to understand news events in your own community, it makes little sense to follow news events from half a world away.

In today's information-based society, it is easier than ever to keep up with world news events. But for the reasons given above, it is better to remain unaware of world news events that have no bearing on your life.

Critical Analysis Refer to the sample response to complete the tasks below.

1 Underline the topic sentence in each paragraph.

2 Double underline the sentences that include supporting details.

3 List some of the examples the writer uses on the lines below.

_____

_____

Revising Use the guided sample response to help you revise your own response to the question. Be sure to incorporate specific vocabulary and phrasing from the guided sample response.

In my opoinion, I agree to keep with world events even if they do not effect your life because know the event is a good thing.

Some peple want to know what happen in the world because they learn about their own home town more greatly. So when they see the news from the world, then they see the news from there communaty. Then they understand the news better. What I mean is that seeing the news about the outside, let's you see better at the inside.

Second the problem of the news can move to the home town. In other words, problem travel quickly. Let me give an example. If someone gets an disease in the other place, they know suddenly show aobut getting the disease. Suddenly the disease is now your country. Without see the news you don't know the disease.

Alos, you must care for the toher peple. Another word for this is emapaty. This is peple care about the another. A great catastrophy happens and you can feel sorry aobut the others. So see this other world can help you become more emapaty.

In conclusion, I believe that keep up with world news is very important for three reasons above.

Evaluation Grade the response by using the grid below. A place to take notes has been provided.

Score	5	4	3	2	1	Notes
Development						
Organization						
Unity						
Language Use				V		

Final Score: _____

Critical Analysis Where could the following sentence be added to strengthen the response?

Seeing news stories about people suffering in other parts of the world might inspire you to improve the lives of others in your own community.

- Ⓐ Body paragraph 1
- Ⓑ Body paragraph 2
- Ⓒ Body paragraph 3

Part

B

Chapter 06

Integrated Writing
◊ Environmental Studies: Green Consumerism

Independent Writing
◊ Spending Money on International Issues

Environmental Studies: Green Consumerism

Vocabulary Take a few moments to review the vocabulary items that will appear in this task.

deforestation *n* the act or process of removing trees from or clearing a forest

Deforestation in the Amazon has contributed substantially to climate change.

avert *v* to ward off something about to happen; to prevent

I **averted** getting in a car accident by slamming on the brakes.

preserve *v* to maintain in safety from injury, peril, or harm; to protect

Opponents of same-sex marriage claim they want to **preserve** the purity of marriage.

landfill *n* a site used for waste disposal

Many **landfills** are converted into parks and zoos once they are filled.

laden *adj* weighed down with a load; heavy

Many people do not drink tap water because they believe it is **laden** with chemicals.

pesticide *n* a chemical used to kill pests, especially insects

Organic vegetables are grown without the use of **pesticides**.

gateway *n* something that serves as an entrance or a means of access

The new park will serve as a **gateway** to the Museum of Modern Art.

domino effect *n* an effect of increasing intensity produced when one event sets off a chain of similar events

The financial crisis in Argentina could create a **domino effect** on financial markets throughout the world.

Reading Read the passage carefully. Be sure to take notes in the margins about the main ideas and the supporting examples from each of the body paragraphs. You have 3 minutes to read.

Margin Notes

In recent years, people have become aware of all of the problems humans have created for the Earth. Faced with issues ranging from ozone depletion to deforestation, people have begun to search for ways to protect the planet. The Green Consumerism Revolution is the answer we need to avert environmental catastrophe.

One of the key advantages of green consumerism is that it is an easy way for average people to help protect the environment. By making small changes to their purchasing habits, consumers can reduce carbon emissions and preserve resources. Products such as blue jeans, which are made from biodegradable cotton, can cut down on waste. These small changes to consumption habits have had far-reaching effects. Studies have shown that green consumerism has reduced landfill waste by nearly ten percent.

Green consumerism also benefits customers directly because many green products are higher quality, more efficient, or healthier than regular products. Compact fluorescent light bulbs last more than five times longer than traditional incandescent bulbs. The latest hybrid sedans get fifteen more miles per gallon on the highway than conventional sedans. And organically grown fruits and vegetables are not laden with the pesticides found in regular produce.

Another important aspect of green consumerism is the fact that it serves as a gateway to other environmental activism. When people purchase green products, they get a sense that they are making an important contribution to protect the environment. As a result, they begin to seek other ways in which they can help. Thus, green consumerism creates a domino effect in which simple changes lead people to take more drastic steps to protect the environment.

Glossary **biodegradable** *adj* something that breaks down or decays naturally without any special scientific treatment and can therefore be thrown away without causing pollution

◈ **Note-Taking** Refer to the reading to complete the outline below.

1 Main Idea of the Passage: ....

....

2 First Supporting Argument: ....

....

3 Second Supporting Argument: ....

....

4 Third Supporting Argument: ....

....

Critical Thinking Consider the following questions. Answer them in complete sentences.

1 What do you think some potential drawbacks of green products are?

2 How can green consumerism actually harm the environment?

Vocabulary Take a few moments to review the vocabulary items that will appear in this task.

misconception *n* a mistaken thought, idea, or notion; a misunderstanding

Citizens had many **misconceptions** about the new tax program.

prevailing *adj* generally current; widespread

It is the **prevailing** scientific consensus that human activity is primarily responsible for global warming.

curb *v* to check, restrain, or control as if with a curb; to rein in

The government has promised to **curb** skyrocketing real estate prices by introducing new laws.

minute *adj* exceptionally small; tiny

Some scientists believe the impact of global warming is so **minute** that it should not even be considered.

complacency *n* a feeling of contentment or self-satisfaction, especially when coupled with an unawareness of danger, trouble, or controversy

The rabbit lost the race to the tortoise after developing a sense of **complacency** about his victory.

sizable *adj* of considerable size; fairly large

Although a **sizable** number of people own smartphone, there are still millions of people who do not have one.

carcinogen *n* a cancer-causing substance or agent

Pesticides contain **carcinogens** and should not be consumed.

◈ **Listening** Now listen to part of a lecture on the topic you just read about.

02-06

◆**Note-Taking** Refer to the listening to complete the outline below.

1 Main Idea of the Lecture:

....

....

2 First Supporting Argument:

....

....

3 Second Supporting Argument:

....

....

4 Third Supporting Argument:

....

....

(**Critical Thinking**) Consider the following questions. Answer them in complete sentences.

1 In what ways does the professor refute the points made in the reading?

2 In what ways does the professor fail to address the arguments made in the reading?

◈**Tandem Note-Taking** Refer to the outlines for the reading and the listening to complete the side-by-side notes below. Include only the three points from the reading and the listening that clearly contradict each other.

Reading	Listening
Main Idea	**Main Idea**
First Supporting Argument	**First Supporting Argument**
Supporting Detail	Supporting Detail
Second Supporting Argument	**Second Supporting Argument**
Supporting Detail	Supporting Detail
Third Supporting Argument	**Third Supporting Argument**
Supporting Detail	Supporting Detail

Scaffolding Here are some useful phrases to help you when you write.

In the listening, the lecturer makes arguments that contradict the…

The lecturer begins by…

He illustrates this by explaining that…

This argument goes against the reading, which says…

The lecturer's second point is…

Again, this contradicts the reading, which says…

The lecturer concludes by refuting the belief that…

His argument calls into question the argument made in the reading that…

◈ Writing Use this page to write your response. You have 20 minutes to complete your essay.

Writing Guide	Summarize the points made in the lecture, being sure to explain how they cast doubt on specific points made in the reading passage.

▶ **First Paragraph**

State and discuss thesis

▶ **Second Paragraph**

First main idea from lecture

Supporting detail

Contradiction from reading

▶ **Third Paragraph**

Second main idea from lecture

Supporting detail

Contradiction from reading

▶ **Fourth Paragraph**

Third main idea from lecture

Supporting detail

Contradiction from reading

▶ **Fifth Paragraph**

Conclusion (optional)

The topic of the reading and the listening is green consumerism. In the listening, the lecturer makes arguments that contradict the points made in the reading.

The lecturer begins by discrediting the notion that people can curb environmental destruction by making only small changes to their shopping habits. He illustrates this by explaining that if every person on the planet bought only green products for a year, it would only reduce pollutants as much as the shutting down of a single power plant for one day. This argument goes against the reading, which says that small changes to buying habits have far-reaching effects on the environment.

Next, the lecturer refutes the belief that green products offer superior performances over those of regular products. He explains that most green products have a hidden cost and illustrates this by mentioning the carcinogens contained in fluorescent light bulbs. This rebuts the argument made in the reading that all green products are better for consumers and the environment.

The lecturer concludes by explaining that green consumerism does not lead people to become more environmentally active and that most green consumers are less likely to recycle or to use alternative energy sources. Again, this contradicts the reading, which says that green consumerism has a domino effect that leads to increased environmentalism.

Critical Analysis Refer to the sample response to complete the tasks below.

1 Underline the topic sentence in each paragraph.

2 Double underline the sentences that refer to the listening.

3 List some of the transitions the writer uses on the lines below.

_____

_____

Revising Use the guided sample response to help you revise your own response on the previous page. Be sure to incorporate specific vocabulary and phrasing from the guided sample response.

The ideas shown in the reading and lecture contradicted very much. The reading said that green consumerism easily allow people to participate in the helping the environtment, but the listening disagree with this. There, it said even if all people stop buying products for a whole year, it would not stop pollution as much as turning off power plants. Also, the reading mention that green products are more beneficial than conventenal products, again the professor disagrees. He says that the befits of green products have a hidden cost, which mean that there more benefits outweights the advantages. Lastly, the listening talked about the green consumerism domino effect. He said that most green consumerism people have a complacency and don't do anything really to help. The only point of correlation between the reading and speech was the fact that some green products are better than regular products.

Evaluation Grade the response by using the grid below. A place to take notes has been provided.

Score	5	4	3	2	1	Notes
Development						
Organization				V		
Unity						
Language Use						

Final Score: _____

Critical Analysis In which of the following ways should the highlighted sentence be rewritten?

(A) The lecturer explains that green products often have hidden costs that outweigh their advantages.

(B) The professor argues that most green products are likely to exclude hidden costs.

(C) According to the lecture, the hidden cost of a conventional product is less consequential than its advantages.

Spending Money on International Issues

Q Do you agree or disagree with the following statement? It is better for governments of rich nations to spend money on international issues rather than on domestic problems. Use specific reasons and details to support your answer.

- -

◈Generating Ideas The following questions will help you write your response. Answer each with one or two sentences. Plan an answer for both options. Some ideas have been provided to help you.

> **Idea Box**
>
> **1** How can spending money on international issues affect relationships between nations?
> **2** Who benefits when rich nations provide assistance to poor nations?
> **3** What are some potential consequences if problems in poor nations go unchecked?

▷ **Agree**

Reason 1:

Reason 2:

Reason 3:

> **Idea Box**
>
> **1** What obligations do nations have to their citizens?
> **2** How could donated money be misused by nations that receive it?
> **3** What reasons might a rich nation have for providing financial assistance beyond giving aid?

▷ **Disagree**

Reason 1:

Reason 2:

Reason 3:

◈Developing Ideas Having examined the two options, which do you feel more comfortable developing into an essay?

Planning Use the outline to plan your response to the following: Do you agree or disagree with the following statement? It is better for governments of rich nations to spend money on international issues rather than on domestic problems. Use specific reasons and details to support your answer.

Thesis Statement (Agree / Disagree) ....

....

First Supporting Idea ....

....

Supporting Example ....

....

Second Supporting Idea ....

....

Supporting Example ....

....

Third Supporting Idea ....

....

Supporting Example ....

....

Conclusion ....

....

Scaffolding Here are some useful phrases to help you when you write.

I feel that nations have an obligation to…

I do not think it is wise to…

Although a rich nation might claim to have good intentions, in reality…

Several aid organizations, including… already exist in the world.

Nowhere is this seen more clearly than with…

By providing international aid, rich nations ultimately benefit…

When rich nations give aid, there is no guarantee that the money will be…

Writing Guide	Do you agree or disagree with the following statement? It is better for governments of rich nations to spend money on international issues rather than on domestic problems. Use specific reasons and details to support your answer.

▸ **First Paragraph**

State and discuss thesis

▸ **Second Paragraph**

First main supporting idea

Supporting detail

Example

▸ **Third Paragraph**

Second main supporting idea

Supporting detail

Example

▸ **Fourth Paragraph**

Third main supporting idea

Supporting detail

Example

▸ **Fifth Paragraph**

Conclusion

Vocabulary Take a few moments to review the vocabulary items that will appear in this response.

rectify *v* to set right; to correct
Before leaving home, I had to **rectify** all of the problems that I had caused.

imperative *adj* impossible to avoid doing; urgent
This button will blow up the whole ship, so it is **imperative** that you do not press it.

prosperous *adj* having success; flourishing
In **prosperous** nations, people enjoy luxuries such as clean drinking water and electricity.

noblesse oblige *n* the obligation of those of high rank to be honorable and generous
Noblesse oblige specifies that a noble act must be returned nobly.

infrastructure *n* the basic facilities needed in a society, such as transportation systems and schools
Many African nations lack the basic **infrastructure** necessary to improve the lives of their citizens.

prowess *n* superior skill or ability
Nathan's writing **prowess** is unsurpassed; he will surely be a famous novelist someday.

recipient *n* one who receives something
The elderly are the most common **recipients** of blood donations.

tackle *v* to engage or to deal with
The government formed a committee to **tackle** the issue of inner-city crime.

In today's integrated global society, it is important for nations to help each other as much as possible. Therefore, I agree with the statement that the governments of rich nations should spend money on international issues rather than on domestic problems.

First, donations from rich nations can prevent international issues from spreading and becoming more serious. As many nations suffering from the worst domestic problems are unable to rectify these issues themselves, it is imperative that rich nations provide financial assistance. If aid is not given, these domestic problems can become more severe. To illustrate, consider the food shortages in North Korea. When rich nations provided aid, the North Korean people were able to subsist. However, now that international aid has been cut off, thousands of North Koreans have been dying from starvation. To end human suffering, rich nations must provide international aid.

In addition to preventing problems from spreading, aid from rich nations can help make all nations of the world prosperous. The concept of noblesse oblige dictates that the rich should help the needy in order to benefit society. The same holds true on a global scale. Rich nations must assist poorer nations in developing infrastructure and improving living standards for their citizens. As poorer nations gain economic prowess, they become important trading partners with the nations that provided them aid. This allows richer nations to develop their own economies while helping the people of less developed nations become wealthy. When rich nations provide aid to poorer nations, both the giver and the recipient benefit.

Some argue that nations should focus on domestic problems before trying to tackle issues abroad. However, for the reasons outlined above, it is clear that rich nations should spend money on international issues rather than on domestic problems.

Critical Analysis Refer to the sample response to complete the tasks below.

1 Underline the topic sentence in each paragraph.

2 Double underline the sentences that include supporting details.

3 List some of the examples the writer uses on the lines below.

_____

_____

Revising Use the guided sample response to help you revise your own response to the question. Be sure to incorporate specific vocabulary and phrasing from the guided sample response.

Although there are people who thinks that spending money on internationel issue is better it is actually most important to spend money on domestic issues. Firstly, governments should support their citicens first, secondly spending money on others makes them angry, finally most governments don't even want the money anyway.

to begin with goverments should support their citizens first because their citizens keep the government floating. For example, since people pay taxes to the govermnet the people should reep the of this. In other words, the governments have responsibility to support the citizens that pay them by provide services like health care and education.

Next giving too much money to other govermnets can revolt to the people. What I mean is giving too much money to abroad can make people feel upset like above. If you consider the issue you know that people won't be happy if goverment gives too much money, like billions of dollars to other nations. This means a revolt where the people get so angry they throw down the government. In short, governments must make the people happy first.

Lastly, the other nations probably don't want the money anyway. Like African nations. These nations are pride of themselves, so they don't need help. Donating money just makes them feel shamed and make the problem worse. Also. the head of these nation maynot use the money rightly anyway because they are corrupt, which means it go to waste. That is to say, donating the money is a waste of time because they can't know if the money is used rightly.

In conclusion, donating money to international problems is not helpfull as the reasons above, so it is better to spend money on domestic issues.

Evaluation Grade the response by using the grid below. A place to take notes has been provided.

Score	5	4	3	2	1	Notes
Development			V			
Organization						
Unity						
Language Use						

Final Score: _____

Critical Analysis Which of the following sentences would best strengthen the response?

Ⓐ Consider the famous phrase "No taxation without representation."

Ⓑ Many African nations have a history of misusing money donated by foreign nations.

Ⓒ Historically, civil unrest has led to revolutions, such as the ones in America and France.

Chapter 07

Integrated Writing
◊ Business: Maintaining U.S. Policies Abroad

Independent Writing
◊ Class Attendance Should Not Be Required

Business: Maintaining U.S. Policies Abroad

Vocabulary Take a few moments to review the vocabulary items that will appear in this task.

uniform *adj* conforming to one principle, standard, or rule; consistent

In order to give all applicants an equal opportunity to be hired, OmniCorp has enacted a **uniform** hiring policy.

subsidiary *n* a company that is controlled by a larger company

This company used to be independent, but now it is a **subsidiary** of Mobile Systems, Inc.

stringent *adj* imposing rigorous standards of performance; severe

To reduce the number of accidents, the company has introduced more **stringent** safety measures.

dictate *v* to prescribe with authority; to impose

Because he had won the previous game, Juan **dictated** some new rules for the next match.

just *adj* suitable or proper in nature; fitting

The murderer received a **just** sentence of life in prison for his terrible crimes.

compensate *v* to make satisfactory payment or reparation to; to reimburse

We were **compensated** for working over the weekend on the project.

backlash *n* an opposing reaction by a group to a trend, development, or event

There was a tremendous **backlash** after the city introduced a smoking ban in all bars and clubs.

child labor *n* the full-time employment of children who are under a minimum legal age

In the 1990s, there was a severe backlash against some companies for using **child labor**.

Reading Read the passage carefully. Be sure to take notes in the margins about the main ideas and the supporting examples from each of the body paragraphs. You have 3 minutes to read.

American multinational corporations have a long-established history. The first such corporation was founded in the early nineteenth century, and their number has risen dramatically since the end of World War II. As these American companies increasingly expand their manufacturing facilities internationally, they must adopt a uniform code of American ethics across all of their subsidiaries.

One of the greatest benefits of such a policy would be increased safety. American safety regulations are among the most stringent in the world and therefore greatly reduce the chance of a serious accident occurring. Failure to maintain this level of safety has often had disastrous results. For example, had the chemical company at Bhopal, India, followed American rather than Indian safety standards, the explosion of its chemical plant in the 1980s would have caused fewer deaths of citizens in the neighboring community.

Enforcing an American code of ethics would also directly benefit employees by providing better working conditions. Although it might be legal in Mexico to employ ten-year-old children to work twelve hours a day weaving rugs, such child labor is prohibited under American labor laws. Additionally, American labor laws dictate that employees receive a just and livable wage, which guarantees that all employees of American

📖 **Margin Notes**

multinationals are fairly compensated.

Companies also benefit from enforcing American policies abroad. Many consumers prefer to buy products from businesses that maintain adequate working conditions for their employees, and the backlash against companies that do not has been severe. Recently, consumers boycotted a famous sneaker company when it was discovered that it used child labor to produce its products, which led the company to adopt American work policies for all of its subsidiaries. In short, companies that adopt a uniform code of ethics are able to improve their reputations and increase their profits.

◈ **Note-Taking** Refer to the reading to complete the outline below.

1 Main Idea of the Passage: ....

....

2 First Supporting Argument: ....

....

3 Second Supporting Argument: ....

....

4 Third Supporting Argument: ....

....

(**Critical Thinking**) Consider the following questions. Answer them in complete sentences.

1 How can the following American policies abroad reduce a company's competitiveness?

2 Do you think all subsidiaries would appreciate having to follow an American code of ethics?

hamper *v* to prevent the free movement, action, or progress of

It would **hamper** the runners if the refreshment stand were located on the track.

adhere *v* to follow a rule or agreement

All employees are required to **adhere** to the company's policies.

comply *v* to follow another's command, request, rule, or wish

The patient **complied** with the doctor's orders.

revenue *n* all of the income produced by a particular source

The game company's **revenue** increased dramatically with the release of its newest game.

in step with *exp* in conformity with; in harmony with

Critics say the president is not **in step with** the needs of the people.

mandate *v* to make something required, as by law; to decree or require

In the 1960s, U.S. courts **mandated** the desegregation of public schools.

ethical imperialism *n* the idea of one culture imposing its values upon another culture

One of the characteristics of colonization is **ethical imperialism**.

alienate *v* to cause to become unfriendly or hostile

If you **alienate** your family, you might regret it when you need their help.

baffle *v* to frustrate or check someone by confusing or perplexing that person; to stymie

To win the game, you must **baffle** your opponent.

clash *v* to come into conflict; to be in opposition

Do not make any policy decisions that **clash** with official company thinking.

◈ **Listening**   Now listen to part of a lecture on the topic you just read about.

02-07

◈ **Note-Taking** Refer to the listening to complete the outline below.

1 Main Idea of the Lecture: ....

....

2 First Supporting Argument: ....

....

3 Second Supporting Argument: ....

....

4 Third Supporting Argument: ....

....

(Critical Thinking) Consider the following questions. Answer them in complete sentences.

1 In what ways does the lecturer refute the points made in the reading?

2 In what ways does the lecturer fail to address the arguments made in the reading?

◈**Tandem Note-Taking** Refer to the outlines for the reading and the listening to complete the side-by-side notes below. Include only the three points from the reading and the listening that clearly contradict each other.

Reading	Listening
Main Idea	**Main Idea**
First Supporting Argument	**First Supporting Argument**
Supporting Detail	Supporting Detail
Second Supporting Argument	**Second Supporting Argument**
Supporting Detail	Supporting Detail
Third Supporting Argument	**Third Supporting Argument**
Supporting Detail	Supporting Detail

Scaffolding Here are some useful phrases to help you when you write.

The reading and the lecture address the topic of…

While the reading supports…the listening strongly opposes it.

The professor begins by explaining…

This counters the argument made in the reading that…

The lecturer then states that…

Again, this refutes the argument made in the reading, which states…

The lecturer concludes by arguing that…

This goes against the argument made in the reading…

◈ **Writing** Use this page to write your response. You have 20 minutes to complete your essay.

Writing Guide	Summarize the points made in the lecture, being sure to explain how they cast doubt on specific points made in the reading passage.

▸ **First Paragraph**

State and discuss thesis

▸ **Second Paragraph**

First main idea from lecture

Supporting detail

Contradiction from reading

▸ **Third Paragraph**

Second main idea from lecture

Supporting detail

Contradiction from reading

▸ **Fourth Paragraph**

Third main idea from lecture

Supporting detail

Contradiction from reading

▸ **Fifth Paragraph**

Conclusion (optional)

The reading and the lecture address the topic of whether to adopt American policies at overseas affiliates. While the reading supports adopting American policies, the lecturer strongly opposes it.

The professor begins by arguing that following American policies reduces the competitiveness of a company. This is illustrated by a cell phone company that was unable to release its products in China because it refused to comply with Chinese policies, so it therefore lost millions of dollars in potential revenue. This counters the argument made in the reading that following American policies at foreign subsidiaries would create safer working environments.

The lecturer then argues that companies lose business by following American policies. For example, one car company paid its Mexican workers the American minimum wage rather than the local minimum wage. By doing this, the company was not able to compete with other manufacturers and consequently had to move its production facilities elsewhere. Again, this refutes the argument made in the reading, which states that following American policies would create better working conditions for employees.

The instructor concludes by arguing that companies that impose American work standards on foreign subsidiaries can alienate their foreign workforce and potential client base. This is explained with the case of an American company that offended its foreign staff by requiring them to take a course on sexual harassment. This goes against the argument made in the reading that enforcing American work standards can improve a company's reputation and increase its profits.

Critical Analysis Refer to the sample response to complete the tasks below.

1 Underline the topic sentence in each paragraph.

2 Double underline the sentences that refer to the listening.

3 List some of the transitions the writer uses on the lines below.

_____

_____

Revising Use the guided sample response to help you revise your own response on the previous page. Be sure to incorporate specific vocabulary and phrasing from the guided sample response.

The lecture gave reasons why American companies should keep US policies in abroad. These ideas went against the ones made in the reading passage.

The professor first presented the argument that companies that don't follow local business policies lose their ability to compete. In the reading, on the other hand, it was argued that American policies increase the safety of a company abroad. But in the lecture, the example of the cell phone company explained why local policies are better.

Next, the lecture argued that Americans need to keep their wages in step with the local companies. What this means is, they can't not pay excessively to their employees. Such was what happened at the Mexican autocompany. The US company paid employees too high salaries, so they were forced to close the operation. This contradicts the reading's idea that the American standards make a better work environment for employees.

Finally, the instructor stated that American companies confuse their foreinger employees. This is because Americans ask them to do tasks they should have to do, like the sexual harasment course explained in the lecture. This is unlike the reading, where it was argued that following local policies is good for business.

Evaluation Grade the response by using the grid below. A place to take notes has been provided.

Score	5	4	3	2	1	Notes
Development						
Organization						
Unity	V					
Language Use						

Final Score: _____

Critical Analysis Which of the following sentences could be added to strengthen the response?

(A) This contradicts the idea presented in the reading that overseas subsidiaries would benefit from following American policies.

(B) The reading argues that employees who follow American safety policies have a greatly reduced chance of dying on the job.

(C) The text states that companies in foreign countries generally adhere to American safety standards.

Class Attendance Should Not Be Required

 Q Do you agree or disagree with the following statement? University students should not be required to attend classes. Taking the final exam or writing a final paper should be the only requirement. Use specific reasons and examples to support your answer.

◈ **Generating Ideas** The following questions will help you write your response. Answer each with one or two sentences. Plan an answer for both options. Some ideas have been provided to help you. Give reasons and examples to support your opinion.

☼ Idea Box

1 How can optional class attendance help students learn to work independently?
2 Generally, how is learning assessed at universities? How does this relate to class attendance?
3 What learning resources are generally available to university students?

▷ **Agree**

Reason 1:

Reason 2:

Reason 3:

☼ Idea Box

1 How can requiring class attendance facilitate learning?
2 What are the drawbacks to only having one assignment determine the grade for a class?
3 In what ways does mandatory class attendance prepare students for the working world?

▷ **Disagree**

Reason 1:

Reason 2:

Reason 3:

◈ **Developing Ideas** Having examined the two options, which do you feel more comfortable developing into an essay?

◈ Planning Use the outline to plan your response to the following: Do you agree or disagree with the following statement? University students should not be required to attend classes. Taking the final exam or writing a final paper should be the only requirement. Use specific reasons and examples to support your answer.

Thesis Statement (Agree / Disagree) ....

....

First Supporting Idea ....

....

Supporting Example ....

....

Second Supporting Idea ....

....

Supporting Example ....

....

Third Supporting Idea ....

....

Supporting Example ....

....

Conclusion ....

....

Scaffolding | Here are some useful phrases to help you when you write.

I believe that class attendance should/should not be...

Most students benefit from a more organized...

One of the best ways to learn is directly from...

To give you an idea, here is an example from my personal...

Because most professors post their class notes online...

Furthermore, students might become too stressed out if...

Some students simply learn better when...

For all of these reasons, I think that...

◆ **Writing** Use this page to write your response. You have 30 minutes to complete your essay.

Writing Guide	Do you agree or disagree with the following statement? University students should not be required to attend classes. Taking the final exam or writing a final paper should be the only requirement. Use specific reasons and examples to support your answer.

▸ **First Paragraph**

State and discuss
thesis

▸ **Second Paragraph**

First main
supporting idea

Supporting detail

Example

▸ **Third Paragraph**

Second main
supporting idea

Supporting detail

Example

▸ **Fourth Paragraph**

Third main
supporting idea

Supporting detail

Example

▸ **Fifth Paragraph**

Conclusion

Vocabulary   Take a few moments to review the vocabulary items that will appear in this response.

structured *adj* having a well-defined structure or organization; organized
I prefer to work in a **structured** work environment.

equitable *adj* fair and impartial
Be sure to share the pie in an **equitable** manner.

glean *v* to gather facts in small quantities
I will read the document carefully and **glean** any information that is useful to me.

feasible *adj* capable of being accomplished or brought about; possible
Your plan is highly ambitious, but I am not sure if it is technically **feasible**.

interval *n* a space of time or a space between things
The subway comes at three-minute **intervals** during rush hour.

pertinent *adj* concerning a subject or connected to it; relevant
The most **pertinent** issue in economics today is the global credit crisis.

allot *v* to give out by shares or to divide
My new job **allots** me fifteen days of vacation each year.

flourish *v* to grow strongly and well
The oak trees **flourished** in the new soil we planted them in.

Some university students feel that they should not be required to attend classes and that grades should only consist of final exams or research essays. However, I believe that class attendance should be mandatory even for university students because it provides a more structured learning environment, makes the grading process more equitable, and prepares students better for the working world.

By making class attendance mandatory, students receive a superior education in a more structured learning environment. This occurs for several reasons. For one, university professors are experts in their fields and are therefore able to provide insight into subjects that students might not be able to glean themselves. Furthermore, as many university students are still fairly immature, mandatory class attendance can help them remain focused on their studies while providing them with a study plan to make learning possible.

In conjunction with making studying more structured, mandatory class attendance also makes the grading process more equitable. For the vast majority of students, placing the entire weight of a class's grade on one exam or essay is neither fair nor feasible. Students would have only one opportunity to demonstrate their learning, and if they did not study properly, they would fail the class. However, mandatory class attendance allows students to test their knowledge at various intervals over the course of a semester and make changes to their study habits as needed. Thus, it is clear that mandatory class attendance gives students more opportunities to succeed.

Another more contemporary aim of universities is to prepare students for the working world. To this end, mandatory class attendance is unquestionably pertinent. Very few jobs allot employees, especially recent graduates, the freedom and the flexibility to work wherever and whenever they want. When the students become employees, they will be expected to work regular hours according to a strict schedule. In this regard, mandatory class attendance better prepares students to enter the working world.

Ours is a world of structure and predictability. We learn and live best by following schedules. And while a minority of students may flourish in a university environment in which class attendance is not mandatory, for the reasons I listed above, I feel that the majority of students learn best when they are required to go to class.

Critical Analysis Refer to the sample response to complete the tasks below.

1 Underline the topic sentence in each paragraph.

2 Double underline the sentences that include supporting details.

3 List some of the examples the writer uses on the lines below.

_____

_____

Revising Use the guided sample response to help you revise your own response to the question. Be sure to incorporate specific vocabulary and phrasing from the guided sample response.

going to the university is a big deal for most people. it is the time when they become adults. since of this i agree that students should not be required to attend the classes for three reasons.

for some student, study outside the class give more learning. in other words, the students should not go to class because they are already good at study. let me give an example, a student who is already excellent at math should not have go to the class because healready knows it. also, the student who read a lot of history books should already know the history, so class is not neccessary.

secondly, most professor just do teaching from textbook. that to say they don't rely on their knowledge just the book. also, they put their notes on the internet any way. which means that even if you don't go to the leckture, you can still know what they have to teach, like the english teacher hwo puts the notes up online and then the study guide. if you see this you aleardy know what to do for the classwork. in the end, going to class is a waste of time because the classwork is already give to you on line.

thirdly, going to the class cannot be demonstrate your knowledge, only tests does that. in university, you have to show your knowledge. so you need to take tests in any instance. this means that when you take a class you already take a test. therefore, why do you need to go to class? if you know what the test has, then its ok. you can't study for class, you only study for test. this means that only tests should be required.

to sum up, i beleve that students should not be required to attend classes because the study outside the class provides more learning, most proessors just teaching text book, and the test must be take in anycase.

Evaluation Grade the response by using the grid below. A place to take notes has been provided.

Score	5	4	3	2	1	Notes
Development						
Organization						
Unity						
Language Use				V		

Final Score: _____

Critical Analysis Which of the main body paragraphs could be combined to strengthen the response?

  (A) Body paragraphs 1 and 3
  (B) Body paragraphs 2 and 3
  (C) Body paragraphs 1 and 2

Chapter 08

Integrated Writing
◊ Computer Science: Are Internet Encyclopedias Better?

Independent Writing
◊ Documentaries and Books

Computer Science: Are Internet Encyclopedias Better?

Vocabulary Take a few moments to review the vocabulary items that will appear in this task.

surge *v* to increase suddenly
As favorable reviews came out, ticket sales for the movie **surged**.

tome *n* a book, especially a large or scholarly one
To do scholarly research, reading many different **tomes** is essential.

hardbound *adj* having a hard back or cover
The **hardbound** version of a novel is always more expensive than the paperback version.

rigorously *adv* done with great or extreme bodily, mental, or spiritual strength
Exercise is of little value unless it is done **rigorously**.

tamper *v* to interfere in a harmful manner
I do not want to be accused of **tampering** with the evidence.

misconstrue *v* to mistake the meaning of; to misinterpret
Please do not **misconstrue** what I said to you.

facet *n* one of numerous aspects, as of a subject
In the Middle Ages, the social class system shaped every **facet** of European life.

trivial *adj* of little significance or value
The president does not have time to deal with **trivial** matters.

◆**Reading** Read the passage carefully. Be sure to take notes in the margins about the main ideas and the supporting examples from each of the body paragraphs. You have 3 minutes to read.

In recent years, the number of people turning to online encyclopedias to gather information has surged dramatically. These digital tomes may be superior to published encyclopedias in some respects, but traditional encyclopedias offer a number of important advantages over their online counterparts.

One of the most important strengths traditional encyclopedias have over online encyclopedias is accuracy. Whereas online encyclopedias can be written and edited by anyone with access to the Internet, hardbound encyclopedias are written only by authorities on the subjects. The information in traditional encyclopedias is rigorously fact-checked by professional scholars who have direct access to pertinent academic sources. This ensures that virtually no errors make their way into the books. As a result, hardbound encyclopedias have a much lower occurrence of inaccuracies than online texts.

Another important advantage of traditional encyclopedias is security. Because it is published in a book, the information in traditional encyclopedias can never be tampered with or misconstrued. Online encyclopedias, in contrast, do not have such security measures. Indeed, the greatest weakness of online encyclopedias is the fact that people who are ignorant or uninformed about a topic can write and edit articles. This can result in information that is inaccurate or misleading. Worse is the constant threat of hackers, who can corrupt and delete this online database.

📖 **Margin Notes**

Furthermore, traditional encyclopedias present only relevant information about a topic. This is due to the fact that authors of traditional encyclopedias are professional writers and scholars who best understand the most important facets of a topic. On the other hand, Internet encyclopedias often emphasize trivial aspects of topics that may lead readers away from the most important concepts about a subject.

◈ **Note-Taking** Refer to the reading to complete the outline below.

1 Main Idea of the Passage: _____

_____

2 First Supporting Argument: _____

_____

3 Second Supporting Argument: _____

_____

4 Third Supporting Argument: _____

_____

(**Critical Thinking**) Consider the following questions. Answer them in complete sentences.

1 How can it be beneficial that virtually anyone can edit online encyclopedias?

2 Do you think traditional encyclopedias or online encyclopedias cover a wider variety of topics? Explain why you feel this way.

Vocabulary Take a few moments to review the vocabulary items that will appear in this task.

relic *n* something that has survived from the past, such as an object, belief, or custom

The rise of the cell phone has made pay phones a **relic** of the past.

ensure *v* to make sure or certain; to insure

In order to **ensure** that the project is completed on time, we will work through the night.

safeguard *n* something that serves as protection or a guard

Taking a second job is a good **safeguard** against unemployment.

misinformation *n* wrong information that is given intentionally

Our spies have been given **misinformation** by the enemy.

dedicated *adj* wholly committed to a particular course of thought or action; devoted

Data Plus is looking for a **dedicated** software developer to join our growing staff.

citation *n* the quoting of an authoritative source for substantiation

Be sure to include **citations** in your research essay.

encryption *n* a type of computer program that makes online data secure

Every banking website features **encryption** to prevent hackers from stealing private information.

Listening Now listen to part of a lecture on the topic you just read about.

02-08

◆ **Note-Taking** Refer to the listening to complete the outline below.

1 Main Idea of the Lecture: ....
  ....

2 First Supporting Argument: ....
  ....

3 Second Supporting Argument: ....
  ....

4 Third Supporting Argument: ....
  ....

(**Critical Thinking**) Consider the following questions. Answer them in complete sentences.

1 In what ways does the professor refute the points made in the reading?

2 In what ways does the professor fail to address the arguments made in the reading?

◆**Tandem Note-Taking** Refer to the outlines for the reading and the listening to complete the side-by-side notes below. Include only the three points from the reading and the listening that clearly contradict each other.

Reading

Main Idea

....

....

First Supporting Argument

....

....

Supporting Detail

....

....

Second Supporting Argument

....

....

Supporting Detail

....

....

Third Supporting Argument

....

....

Supporting Detail

....

....

Listening

Main Idea

....

....

First Supporting Argument

....

....

Supporting Detail

....

....

Second Supporting Argument

....

....

Supporting Detail

....

....

Third Supporting Argument

....

....

Supporting Detail

....

....

Scaffolding | Here are some useful phrases to help you when you write.

The lecturer's argument that… contradicts the reading passage's claim that…

He contrasts this with…

This argument challenges the reading's assertion that…

The professor goes on to explain that…

He illustrates this by mentioning…

He also argues that…

These points go against the reading, which says that…

This is in opposition to the reading passage's claim that…

♦ **Writing** Use this page to write your response. You have 20 minutes to complete your essay.

Writing Guide	Summarize the points made in the lecture, being sure to explain how they challenge specific arguments made in the reading passage.

▸ **First Paragraph**

State and discuss thesis

▸ **Second Paragraph**

First main idea from lecture

Supporting detail

Contradiction from reading

▸ **Third Paragraph**

Second main idea from lecture

Supporting detail

Contradiction from reading

▸ **Fourth Paragraph**

Third main idea from lecture

Supporting detail

Contradiction from reading

▸ **Fifth Paragraph**

Conclusion (optional)

The lecturer discusses some of the characteristics of online encyclopedias. His argument that Internet encyclopedias are superior to traditional encyclopedias contradicts the reading passage's claim that traditional encyclopedias are superior to online ones.

First of all, the lecturer explains that while online encyclopedias may have more errors than hardbound texts, they have their own advantage of changeability. He contends that because traditional encyclopedias are only edited by a small number of people, errors contained in them can go unchecked for several years. He contrasts this with Internet encyclopedias. Because they can be edited immediately, their errors get removed quickly. This argument challenges the reading's assertion that online encyclopedias contain numerous inaccuracies.

The professor goes on to explain that Internet encyclopedias have safeguards to prevent the spread of misinformation. He illustrates this by mentioning that online encyclopedias have fact checkers who delete information in articles that is inaccurate or otherwise not correct. He also mentions that online encyclopedias have powerful encryption to stop the threat of hackers corrupting the site. These points go against the reading, which says that Internet encyclopedias lack security measures to prevent tampering.

Lastly, the instructor argues that the wider variety of topics covered in online encyclopedias is one of their greatest strengths over hardbound encyclopedias. He explains that readers can research virtually any subject that interests them, including famous video games and subways. This is in opposition to the reading passage's claim that online encyclopedias only emphasize trivial aspects of topics.

Critical Analysis Refer to the sample response to complete the tasks below.

1 Underline the topic sentence in each paragraph.

2 Double underline the sentences that refer to the listening.

3 List some of the transitions the writer uses on the lines below.

_____

_____

Revising Use the guided sample response to help you revise your own response on the previous page. Be sure to incorporate specific vocabulary and phrasing from the guided sample response.

The lecture followed the paragraph about encyclopedias, gave some supporting idea about the online encyclopedias.

Firstly, the paragraph said that the traditional encyclopedias have no error because they are edit by scholars, but it was said in the lecutre the complete oppisite: in online encyclopedias have errors fixed more quickly. This is because the online encyclopedia have many editor to fix the errors, but this is not like the traditional encyclopedis where errors stay for many years.

Secondly, the paragraph say that traditional encyclopedia have greater accuracy, but the listening say that have safe guards, too. This is because the internet encyclopedias have schoarls to check the quality of material. Additionally, internet encyclopedis also cannot easily be hacked because of incription. This shows that paragraph is wrong about internet encyclopedias.

Lastly, paragraph said that traditionel encyclopedia present the pertenent information only, unlike the in the lecture, which said online encyclopedias that have many differ subjects. It was said that this is actually the greatest benefit of the online encyclopedia.

Evaluation Grade the response by using the grid below. A place to take notes has been provided.

Score	5	4	3	2	1	Notes
Development						
Organization	V					
Unity						
Language Use						

Final Score: _____

Critical Analysis Which of the following information could be added to strengthen the response?

Ⓐ A detailed explanation of the safeguards online encyclopedias have against hackers

Ⓑ The professional backgrounds of editors of traditional encyclopedias

Ⓒ A brief list of topics covered in online encyclopedias that are not found in hardbound texts

Documentaries and Books

 Q Do you agree or disagree with the following statement? People can learn as much from watching documentaries as they can from reading books. Use specific reasons and examples to support your answer.

◈ **Generating Ideas** The following questions will help you write your response. Answer each with one or two sentences. Plan an answer for both options. Some ideas have been provided to help you.

⭐ Idea Box

1 Why do people like documentaries?
2 How do documentaries help people learn?
3 Why are documentaries appropriate for some people?

▷ **Agree**

Reason 1:

Reason 2:

Reason 3:

⭐ Idea Box

1 Why can people learn more from books than from documentaries?
2 What are the objectives of books in comparison to the objectives of documentaries?
3 How is the writing in books important with regard to learning?

▷ **Disagree**

Reason 1:

Reason 2:

Reason 3:

◈ **Developing Ideas** Having examined the two options, which do you feel more comfortable developing into an essay?

◈ Planning

Use the outline to plan your response to the following: Do you agree or disagree with the following statement? People can learn as much from watching documentaries as they can from reading books. Use specific reasons and examples to support your answer.

Thesis Statement (Agree / Disagree) ....

....

First Supporting Idea ....

....

Supporting Example ....

....

Second Supporting Idea ....

....

Supporting Example ....

....

Third Supporting Idea ....

....

Supporting Example ....

....

Conclusion ....

....

Scaffolding | Here are some useful phrases to help you when you write.

I simply believe/do not believe the statement…

The first reason that I agree/disagree is that…

I learned so much more from the… than I did from the…

The second reason that I agree/disagree is that…

For instance, I am a huge fan of…

They are usually…, but I almost never…

The third reason that I agree/disagree is that…

It is obvious that… are… than…

Writing Guide	Do you agree or disagree with the following statement? People can learn as much from watching documentaries as they can from reading books. Use specific reasons and examples to support your answer.

▸ **First Paragraph**

State and discuss thesis

▸ **Second Paragraph**

First main supporting idea

Supporting detail

Example

▸ **Third Paragraph**

Second main supporting idea

Supporting detail

Example

▸ **Fourth Paragraph**

Third main supporting idea

Supporting detail

Example

▸ **Fifth Paragraph**

Conclusion

Vocabulary   Take a few moments to review the vocabulary items that will appear in this response.

last *v* to take up a certain amount of time
According to the paper, the movie **lasts** for almost two hours.

check out *v* to borrow something from a library
She likes to **check out** books from the library every weekend.

cover *v* to include, deal with, or provide information about
The professor will **cover** the Middle Ages in the next two classes.

objective *n* a goal that a person sets
The **objective** of the game is to score more points than the other team.

primarily *adv* mainly; for the most part
They are **primarily** interested in having a good time on their vacation at the beach.

entertain *v* to amuse; to delight
Clowns **entertain** the audience in between the acts at the circus.

appropriate *adj* suitable or fitting for a certain purpose
You must be sure to wear **appropriate** clothes when you have your job interview.

I simply do not believe the statement is true. There is no way anyone can learn as much from watching documentaries as they can from reading books for a wide variety of reasons. I therefore strongly disagree with the statement.

The first reason that I disagree is that books contain so much more information than documentaries do. Recently, I watched a documentary about volcanoes. It was pretty interesting, and it was based on a book that had been published. However, the documentary only lasted for an hour. I went to the library and checked out the book the documentary was based on. I simply could not believe how much information the book contained. The documentary had only covered a small amount of information. I learned so much more from the book than I did from the documentary.

The second reason that I disagree is that authors write their books with the objective of getting their readers to learn whereas documentary makers are primarily trying to entertain their audience. You cannot learn much when the primary goal is to be entertained. For instance, I am a huge fan of astronomy. I have seen plenty of documentaries on space. They are usually well produced and have great graphics, but I almost never learn from them despite the fact that they look good. I have also read many books on space. These books were written to educate people on space, so I always learn when I read them.

The third reason that I disagree is that many books are written at a high level while documentaries are often made with children in mind. For example, I saw a documentary on lions last week. It was for kids, so it contained no information that I did not already know. On the other hand, there are books that are available for people of all learning levels. There are books for elementary school children, high schoolers, college students, and adults. Because they are the appropriate level for people, the individuals who read these books can learn a lot from them.

It is obvious that books are more educational than documentary. Books contain more information than documentaries, they are not made for entertainment, and they are not made for children like most documentaries are. I therefore disagree with the statement.

Critical Analysis Refer to the sample response to complete the tasks below.

1 Underline the topic sentence in each paragraph.

2 Double underline the sentences that include supporting details.

3 List some of the examples the writer uses on the lines below.

_____

_____

Revising Use the guided sample response to help you revise your own response to the question. Be sure to incorporate specific vocabulary and phrasing from the guided sample response.

There are many people who love to watch documentaries while there are also some who enjoy reading books. I am actually a big fan of both of them.

In my free time, I love channel surfing and then finding documentaries that I can watch. In just the past week, I saw documentaries on art in the Renaissance, ancient Egypt, and the Amazon River. I was utterly amazed by what I was able to learn by watching the documentaries. I was so impressed that I spoke about the documentaries to my friends, and then we decided to try to watch more documentaries on similar topics together. I find that this is a recurring theme in my life. I watch a documentary about a topic that I had not previously thought much about, and then I become interested in it. As a result, I attempt to find out as much as I can about it.

On the other hand, I love borrowing books from the library on a wide variety of topics. Currently, I am reading a novel, a book on Stonehenge, and another book on the Crusades in Europe. All of them—even the novel—are educating me a great deal. I try to read multiple books at the same time, and I also like to make sure that I read one book every week. In addition to my schooling, this allows me to improve my education a great deal.

To conclude, I believe that both documentaries and books are educational and that people need to watch more documentaries and read more books. By doing so, they will become highly educated individuals.

Evaluation Grade the response by using the grid below. A place to take notes has been provided.

Score	5	4	3	2	1	Notes
Development						
Organization						
Unity						
Language Use			V			

Final Score: _____

Critical Analysis What are the main shortcomings of this response?

Ⓐ It uses improper language as well as poor grammar.

Ⓑ It fails to provide enough personal examples.

Ⓒ It does not agree or disagree with the statement in the question.

Chapter 09

Integrated Writing
◊ Archaeology: Is the Sphinx Actually Ancient?

Independent Writing
◊ Reading a Book a Second Time Is More Interesting

Archaeology: Is the Sphinx Actually Ancient?

Vocabulary Take a few moments to review the vocabulary items that will appear in this task.

monument *n* a structure, such as a building or sculpture, erected as a memorial

The Washington **Monument** is the tallest sculpture in the District of Columbia.

contentious *adj* controversial

The election of Arnold Schwarzenegger as California's governor was highly **contentious**.

theory *n* an explanation of how or why something happens, especially one based on scientific study

After an apple fell on his head, Sir Isaac Newton developed the **theory** of gravity.

adorn *v* to enhance or decorate with or as if with ornaments

Each year, my family **adorns** our house with Christmas lights and other festive decorations.

headdress *n* a covering or ornament for the head

Native Americans are known for wearing elaborate **headdresses** during traditional ceremonies.

hypothesis *n* something not proven but considered to be true for the purpose of further investigation

The best way to test your **hypothesis** is to conduct experiments.

tombstone *n* a stone that is used to mark a grave

Each month, we lay flowers upon my father's **tombstone**.

depict *v* to represent in words; to describe

In his novels, Neil Gaiman **depicts** wonderful worlds of fantasy.

erosion *n* a wearing away

The waves cause **erosion** as they hit the beach.

prolong *v* to extend in time or duration

There are fears that falling consumer demand might **prolong** the economic recession.

Reading Read the passage carefully. Be sure to take notes in the margins about the main ideas and the supporting examples from each of the body paragraphs. You have 3 minutes to read.

📖 Margin Notes

One of the most famous sculptural wonders of the ancient world is the Great Sphinx of Giza, located on the west bank of the Nile River in Egypt. The true origins of the monument have long been contentious. However, newly discovered findings suggest that the Sphinx was constructed during the Old Kingdom by the Pharaoh Khafre. Several pieces of evidence support this theory.

The first piece of evidence dating the Sphinx to the Old Kingdom is the statue's facial features. As with other sphinxes produced during that period, the Great Sphinx features a man's head adorned with an ancient Egyptian headdress. Furthermore, Egyptologists have determined that the face of the Sphinx was modeled after none other than Pharaoh Khafre himself.

The Old Kingdom hypothesis is also supported by the tombstone situated between the front paws of the statue. Inscribed on the stone is a story depicting the history of the Old Kingdom. The tale concludes by explaining that the Sphinx was constructed as the guardian angel of the Old Kingdom and that it must be preserved in order to maintain peace. This explanation is supported by the fact that the Sphinx guards the entrance of the second pyramid, which was also constructed by Pharaoh Khafre.

Perhaps the strongest evidence is the amount of erosion on the Sphinx. Originally, the Sphinx had a smooth outer surface that has since worn away due to prolonged exposure to wind and rain. Leading archaeologists and geologists have examined the weathering evident on the Sphinx and compared it to the erosion on the Great Pyramids constructed during Khafre's reign. They concluded that the amount of weathering on the Sphinx is similar to that of other monuments known to be constructed during the Old Kingdom.

Glossary **archaeologist** *n* a person who studies past human life and culture
geologist *n* a person who studies the structure of the Earth

◈ **Note-Taking** Refer to the reading to complete the outline below.

1 Main Idea of the Passage: ....

....

2 First Supporting Argument: ....

....

3 Second Supporting Argument: ....

....

4 Third Supporting Argument: ....

....

(Critical Thinking) Consider the following questions. Answer them in complete sentences.

1 Why might the current appearance of the Sphinx fail to provide evidence about the time of its construction?

2 Do you feel the legend inscribed on the tombstone supports the Old Kingdom theory? Explain why you feel this way.

Vocabulary
Take a few moments to review the vocabulary items that will appear in this task.

hieroglyph *n* a symbol from ancient Egyptian picture writing

Archaeologists were not able to read **hieroglyphs** until the discovery of the Rosetta Stone.

disproportionately *adv* overly large for the situation in size, shape, or amount

Unemployment has a **disproportionately** penalizing effect on disabled people.

leftover *adj* remaining; excess

Please put the **leftover** sandwiches in the refrigerator.

ascension *n* the act of rising or moving upward

The team witnessed its **ascension** from stardom to superstardom after winning the World Series.

annually *adv* recurring, done, or performed every year; yearly

I visit my doctor **annually** for my physical examination.

meteorological *adj* related to the study of weather and weather conditions

Each summer, the **meteorological** society meets to discuss the upcoming hurricane season.

millennium *n* a period of one thousand years

According to the Bible, Jesus Christ lived around two **millennia** ago.

◊ Listening
Now listen to part of a lecture on the topic you just read about.

02-09

◈ **Note-Taking** Refer to the listening to complete the outline below.

1 Main Idea of the Lecture: ....

....

2 First Supporting Argument: ....

....

3 Second Supporting Argument: ....

....

4 Third Supporting Argument: ....

....

(Critical Thinking) Consider the following questions. Answer them in complete sentences.

1 In what ways does the professor refute the points made in the reading?

2 What examples does the professor provide to support her arguments?

◆**Tandem Note-Taking** Refer to the outlines for the reading and the listening to complete the side-by-side notes below. Include only the three points from the reading and the listening that clearly contradict each other.

Reading

Main Idea

....

....

First Supporting Argument

....

....

Supporting Detail

....

....

Second Supporting Argument

....

....

Supporting Detail

....

....

Third Supporting Argument

....

....

Supporting Detail

....

....

Listening

Main Idea

....

....

First Supporting Argument

....

....

Supporting Detail

....

....

Second Supporting Argument

....

....

Supporting Detail

....

....

Third Supporting Argument

....

....

Supporting Detail

....

....

Scaffolding Here are some useful phrases to help you when you write.

The professor believes that… presenting evidence regarding…

Her arguments cast doubt on the claims made in…

This challenges the reading's assertion that…

Next, the lecturer explains that…

She illustrates this by mentioning…

Finally, the instructor discusses…

The lecturer notes that… and concludes that…

This effectively rebuts the reading passage's claim that…

◈ Writing Use this page to write your response. You have 20 minutes to complete your essay.

Writing Guide	Summarize the points made in the lecture, being sure to explain how they challenge specific claims made in the reading passage.

▸ **First Paragraph**

State and discuss thesis

▸ **Second Paragraph**

First main idea from lecture

Supporting detail

Contradiction from reading

▸ **Third Paragraph**

Second main idea from lecture

Supporting detail

Contradiction from reading

▸ **Fourth Paragraph**

Third main idea from lecture

Supporting detail

Contradiction from reading

▸ **Fifth Paragraph**

Conclusion (optional)

The instructor believes that the Great Sphinx of Giza was constructed prior to the Old Kingdom and presents evidence regarding the Sphinx's facial structure, tombstone, and erosion to support this. Her arguments cast doubt on the claims made in the reading passage.

First, the lecturer talks about the history of the Sphinx's face. She explains that the current face on the Sphinx may be a later reconstruction due to the fact that archaeologists have discovered hieroglyphs showing the Sphinx with a lion's head. This challenges the reading passage's assertion that the human head currently on the Sphinx dates it to the Old Kingdom.

Next, the professor explains the history of the tombstone at the front of the Sphinx. She says that the stone was actually built several centuries after the Sphinx. Furthermore, the legend depicted on the stone was created by a later pharaoh to justify his ascension to the throne. This calls into question the reading passage's argument that the Sphinx was constructed to protect the Old Kingdom.

Finally, the lecturer discusses the erosion on the Sphinx. She mentions that the weathering on the statue is the result of heavy rainfall and concludes that the Sphinx must have been constructed during the Early Dynastic Period. This rebuts the reading passage's claim that the erosion on the Sphinx is similar to that of the pyramids constructed during the Old Kingdom.

Critical Analysis Refer to the sample response to complete the tasks below.

1 Underline the topic sentence in each paragraph.

2 Double underline the sentences that refer to the listening.

3 List some of the transitions the writer uses on the lines below.

_____

_____

Revising Use the guided sample response to help you revise your own response on the previous page. Be sure to incorporate specific vocabulary and phrasing from the guided sample response.

The Sphinx has a controvsersal history. It was explained in the reading it was builded during Old Kingdom. However, it was said in the lecture that Sphinx might actually be from another kingdom.

To begin with, the reading says that Sphinx's face has a man on it. For example, it wears the headdress, like the Old Kingdom style. However, in the lecture it was said that old face was maybe a lion. So maybe the face, was construct before Old Kingdom. So perhaps the face is not good evendence to support the theory.

Furthermore, the Sphinx includes the tombstone. This talks the history of the Sphinx. In reading it was explain that a pharoh builded it for himself to make him more popular. However, the lecture said the history of Sphinx may not be known because the tombstone can be wrong. In this way, the tombstone can not be trusted.

At the last point, in the text it was explain that Sphinx was damage because of heavy rain fall. This is unlike which was explain in listening. There, it said some people think it was builded during old kingdom, so the controversy does continue.

Evaluation Grade the response by using the grid below. A place to take notes has been provided.

Score	5	4	3	2	1	Notes
Development						
Organization			V			
Unity						
Language Use						

Final Score: _____

Critical Analysis Which of the following information does the response fail to include?

Ⓐ The current head on the Sphinx is a later reconstruction.

Ⓑ The erosion on the Sphinx must have occurred before the Old Kingdom.

Ⓒ The legend inscribed on the tombstone may not be historically accurate.

Reading a Book a Second Time Is More Interesting

 Q Do you agree or disagree with the following statement? Reading a book a second time is more interesting than reading it the first time. Use reasons and examples to support your answer.

◈ **Generating Ideas** The following questions will help you write your response. Answer each with one or two sentences. Plan an answer for both options. Some ideas have been provided to help you.

Idea Box

1 How can understanding the characters and the plot of a novel help you enjoy it more?
2 In what ways does rereading a novel allow you to better understand it?
3 What specific aspects of a novel can be enjoyed repeatedly?

▷ **Agree**

Reason 1:

Reason 2:

Reason 3:

Idea Box

1 How does knowing the outcome make a novel less interesting?
2 How can rereading a novel make it more difficult to concentrate on its story?
3 In what ways can reading a novel twice be a waste of time?

▷ **Disagree**

Reason 1:

Reason 2:

Reason 3:

◈ **Developing Ideas** Having examined the two options, which do you feel more comfortable developing into an essay?

◈ **Planning** Use the outline to plan your response to the following: Do you agree or disagree with the following statement? Reading a book a second time is more interesting than reading it the first time. Use reasons and examples to support your answer.

Thesis Statement (Agree / Disagree) ....

....

First Supporting Idea ....

....

Supporting Example ....

....

Second Supporting Idea ....

....

Supporting Example ....

....

Third Supporting Idea ....

....

Supporting Example ....

....

Conclusion ....

....

Scaffolding Here are some useful phrases to help you when you write.

That is why I agree with the statement that…

Because I already read the novel, I could/could not…

Complex novels are meant to be read…

For instance, in high school, I had to read…

Rereading a novel also allows me to…

Although/Because I know the outcome of…

All things considered, I believe it is much more/not nearly as enjoyable to…

◈ Writing Use this page to write your response. You have 30 minutes to complete your essay.

Writing Guide	Do you agree or disagree with the following statement? Reading a book a second time is more interesting than reading it the first time. Use reasons and examples to support your answer.

▸ **First Paragraph**

State and discuss thesis

▸ **Second Paragraph**

First main supporting idea

Supporting detail

Example

▸ **Third Paragraph**

Second main supporting idea

Supporting detail

Example

▸ **Fourth Paragraph**

Third main supporting idea

Supporting detail

Example

▸ **Fifth Paragraph**

Conclusion

Vocabulary Take a few moments to review the vocabulary items that will appear in this response.

savor *v* to appreciate fully; to enjoy or relish
I want to **savor** this moment of my great accomplishment.

narrative *n* a story
The **narrative** changed depending on who was telling it.

gripping *adj* catching and holding one's full attention
The novel was truly **gripping**; I could not put it down.

exchange *n* a dialog; a conversation
Christmas dinner was nearly ruined by the angry **exchange** between my aunt and uncle.

antagonist *n* the character who opposes the hero in a novel or drama
In *The Dark Knight*, Batman is the protagonist while the Joker is the **antagonist**.

veil *v* to conceal; to disguise
Heavy fog **veiled** the city's skyline.

ripe *adj* fully developed or mature and ready to be eaten or used
The time is always **ripe** to do the right thing.

ostensibly *adv* on the surface; apparently
Jack was **ostensibly** a college student, but in actuality, he was our new manager.

lineage *n* direct descent from a particular ancestor; family history
The Shoemaker family is able to trace its **lineage** all the way back to the 1600s.

remorse *n* a deep, often painful regret for past wrongs
Remorse often motivates people to correct their mistakes.

I feel that there is no better way to spend a lazy Sunday afternoon than curled up with a good book even if it is one I have read before. In my opinion, novels are pieces of art meant to be savored over and over again. That is why I agree with the statement that reading a book a second time is more interesting than reading it the first time.

When I reread a novel, I can enjoy the story more. The reason is that I already have an understanding of the setting, the plot, and the characters, so I am able to focus more on the relationships between the characters and how they relate to the overall narrative. This is certainly the case with highly complex novels. One such example is Leo Tolstoy's *War and Peace*, which contains dozens of characters, each with his or her own story arc. To fully appreciate a work of this scale, I feel a second reading is essential.

Rereading a novel also allows me to revisit my favorite parts of the story. This is most evident with scenes that are particularly well written and emotionally gripping. In the novel *No Country for Old Men* by Cormac McCarthy, one scene features an exchange between the antagonist and the owner of a small country gas station. The dialog between the men, with the villain making thinly veiled threats against the owner's life, is rife with dramatic tension. Although I know the outcome of this exchange, the tension and the fear generated by the dialog make me want to read it over and over again.

Finally, by revisiting the novel, I am able to understand the work more deeply. Many of the best novels are laden with metaphors and symbolism that only become apparent upon a second or even third reading. This is the case with the William Faulkner story *The Bear*. Ostensibly a hunting narrative, the true purpose of the story is to explain the guilt the main character has about his lineage and the remorse he feels after slaying the bear, which represents man's destruction of nature.

Certain pieces of writing, such as newspaper headlines, magazine articles, and Internet blogs, are meant to be read only once. But novels, with their depth of characterization and scope, are meant to be read repeatedly. All things considered, I believe it is much more enjoyable to read a novel a second time than it is the first time.

Critical Analysis Refer to the sample response to complete the tasks below.

1 Underline the topic sentence in each paragraph.

2 Double underline the sentences that include supporting details.

3 List some of the examples the writer uses on the lines below.

_____

_____

Revising Use the guided sample response to help you revise your own response to the question. Be sure to incorporate specific vocabulary and phrasing from the guided sample response.

The world is filled of novels. There are millions and millions of novels to read. Because of this, you have wonder. Why should you reread a novel again? For the three reasons below, I don't think it is better to read a book second time.

First of all, most novels are not too fun read again. When you read a novel, a second time, you all ready know the characters and plot, so it cannot have excitement. For instance, when you watch a movie you saw again, it is not as exciting. So you become bored quickly and think, I'm wasting my time. If something is not interesting, why should you bother doing it? In short, you shouldn't. The same is the case with reading books again, too.

Second of all, most books aren't suppose to be read two times. Maybe there exceptions, but for most of the time, books expect that the reader hasn't read it before. For example, think about mystery novels. The only reason to read that kind of book is to find out how it ends. However, when you reread it, you know how it ends, and therefore the excitement disappears. This is the problem of reading books twice.

Finally, there are too many books in the world, so why brother reading a book again. Each year millions of new books are made and people have to fight to read them all, even if you read three books a week you only can read 150 books a year. In order to enjoy as much books as possible, you should read only books that are new to you.

Some people may believe that it is better to reread a book a second time, but for the arguments given above, I feel it is better to read books only one time.

Evaluation Grade the response by using the grid below. A place to take notes has been provided.

Score	5	4	3	2	1	Notes
Development						
Organization		V				
Unity						
Language Use						

Final Score: _____

Critical Analysis Which of the main body paragraphs could be combined to strengthen the response?

Ⓐ Body paragraphs 1 and 2

Ⓑ Body paragraphs 2 and 3

Ⓒ Body paragraphs 1 and 3

Chapter 10

Integrated Writing
◊ Chemistry: The Problems Caused by Sulfur Dioxide

Independent Writing
◊ Higher Education Is Only for Good Students

Chemistry: The Problems Caused by Sulfur Dioxide

Vocabulary Take a few moments to review the vocabulary items that will appear in this task.

combustion *n* the process of burning
Is that an internal **combustion** engine?

primary *adj* first in order or importance
Your **primary** task is to enter the base secretly; your secondary task is to turn off the security cameras.

perceptible *adj* capable of being seen; noticeable
Following his trip to Africa, there was a **perceptible** change in his attitude.

lingering *adj* continuing for a long time; prolonged
The winter storm from last weekend is still **lingering** over the area.

congestion *n* the state of being tightly compacted
Traffic **congestion** was so bad that Felix decided to work from home.

omnipresent *adj* existent in all places at all times
An **omnipresent** fog hung over the town.

droplet *n* a tiny amount of water
The **droplets** of rainwater came together to form a thunderstorm.

wreak *v* to cause to happen; to occur as a consequence
The hurricane will **wreak** havoc upon our house unless we prepare for the storm.

acute *adj* extremely sharp or severe; intense
The patient suffered **acute** pain after the operation.

aggravate *v* to make worse or more troublesome
You must rest for three days, or you will **aggravate** your leg injury.

Reading Read the passage carefully. Be sure to take notes in the margins about the main ideas and the supporting examples from each of the body paragraphs. You have 3 minutes to read.

Sulfur dioxide is a gas that can occur both naturally and be manmade. Volcanic eruptions, wildfires, fossil fuel combustion, and heavy industry are some of its primary sources. In recent years, efforts have been made to reduce the amount of sulfur dioxide released into the atmosphere due to its harmful effects on living creatures and the environment.

One of the most perceptible consequences of sulfur dioxide is smog. Sulfur dioxide aerosol gets trapped in the lower levels of the atmosphere, where it creates a lingering haze that greatly reduces visibility, especially in large cities with high traffic congestion. This omnipresent fog presents dangers both physical and psychological. Research shows that vehicular accidents increase by nearly twenty percent on especially smoggy days while the dirty surroundings created by smog can result in depression.

Another problem created by sulfur dioxide is acid rain. Sulfur dioxide mixes with water vapor in the air to produce sulfuric acid, which ultimately returns to the Earth in the form of acid rain. These acidic water droplets wreak havoc upon the environment by destroying crops, by polluting smaller bodies of water, and by damaging buildings and other structures. The problems created by acid rain are especially acute in developing nations and other areas with large numbers of industrial facilities.

Most troubling are the health problems created by inhaling sulfur dioxide. Being exposed to sulfur dioxide for as little as five minutes can

📖 **Margin Notes**

aggravate asthma, cause respiratory difficulties, and require emergency room visits and hospitalization. The reason is that sulfur dioxide reduces the ability of the lungs to resist diseases and illnesses, such as bronchitis and emphysema.

Glossary **aerosol** *n* a gas that contains tiny solid and liquid particles
asthma *n* a disease of the lungs that causes coughing and breathing difficulties
respiratory *adj* related to respiration or the act of breathing

◈ **Note-Taking** Refer to the reading to complete the outline below.

1 Main Idea of the Passage: ....
....

2 First Supporting Argument: ....
....

3 Second Supporting Argument: ....
....

4 Third Supporting Argument: ....
....

(**Critical Thinking**) Consider the following questions. Answer them in complete sentences.

1 Do you think smog can ever be beneficial for the environment? Explain why you feel this way.

2 Who do you think most typically becomes sick after being exposed to sulfur dioxide?

overlook *v* to fail to notice or consider; to miss

When most people look at artwork, they tend to **overlook** the finer details in the paintings.

reflect *v* to throw or bend back light

The mirror on the wall **reflects** my image.

emission *n* a substance discharged into the air, especially due to an internal combustion engine

To reduce carbon dioxide **emissions** from buses, the city has turned to alternative energy sources.

regional *adj* of or relating to a particular area or district

I could not understand Samantha because of her strong **regional** accent.

scapegoat *n* a person who is blamed for something he or she did not do; a victim

Jewish people were made **scapegoats** by Nazi Germans.

emit *v* to give or send out matter or energy

Stoves cook food by **emitting** great amounts of heat.

purportedly *adv* assumed to be such; supposedly

Although there is no clear evidence, the painting is **purportedly** the work of Vincent van Gogh.

document *v* to support a claim with evidence

Only **documented** claims with be considered.

elderly *n* people who are past middle age and nearing old age

Every weekend, my brother and I volunteer to help out the **elderly** in our community.

terminally ill *n* people who are very sick and not expected to live long

Leading doctors are asking that the **terminally ill** be able to end their lives if they choose.

◊ **Listening** Now listen to part of a lecture on the topic you just read about.

02-10

◈ **Note-Taking** Refer to the listening to complete the outline below.

1 Main Idea of the Lecture: _____

_____

2 First Supporting Argument: _____

_____

3 Second Supporting Argument: _____

_____

4 Third Supporting Argument: _____

_____

(**Critical Thinking**) Consider the following questions. Answer them in complete sentences.

1 In what ways does the instructor refute the points made in the reading?

2 In what ways does the instructor fail to address the arguments made in the reading?

◈Tandem Note-Taking

Refer to the outlines for the reading and the listening to complete the side-by-side notes below. Include only the three points from the reading and the listening that clearly contradict each other.

Reading

Main Idea

First Supporting Argument

Supporting Detail

Second Supporting Argument

Supporting Detail

Third Supporting Argument

Supporting Detail

Listening

Main Idea

First Supporting Argument

Supporting Detail

Second Supporting Argument

Supporting Detail

Third Supporting Argument

Supporting Detail

The passage and the lecture deal with…

By examining research that… the professor argues that…

First of all, the lecturer mentions that…

This casts doubt on the reading passage's claim that…

The professor also argues that…

He illustrates this by mentioning…

Finally, the instructor discusses…

He goes on to explain that… and that…

This rebuts the reading passage's claim that…

◆ **Writing** Use this page to write your response. You have 20 minutes to complete your essay.

Writing Guide	Summarize the points made in the lecture, being sure to explain how they cast doubt on specific claims made in the reading passage.

▸ **First Paragraph**

State and discuss thesis

▸ **Second Paragraph**

First main idea from lecture

Supporting detail

Contradiction from reading

▸ **Third Paragraph**

Second main idea from lecture

Supporting detail

Contradiction from reading

▸ **Fourth Paragraph**

Third main idea from lecture

Supporting detail

Contradiction from reading

▸ **Fifth Paragraph**

Conclusion (optional)

The passage and the lecture deal with the problems created by sulfur dioxide. By examining research that environmentalists tend to overlook, the lecturer argues that sulfur dioxide may not be as harmful as the reading passage suggests.

First of all, the lecturer mentions that having some aerosols in the atmosphere is beneficial. He explains that the aerosols reflect sunlight back into space, which helps cool the Earth. He illustrates this by saying that the reduction in sulfur dioxide emissions has led to warming in some parts of the world. This casts doubt on the reading passage's claim that aerosols are strictly harmful.

The instructor also argues that sulfur dioxide is not one of the primary chemicals in acid rain. He says that acid rain is primarily caused by nitrogen oxide and carbon dioxide emitted from automobiles. This argument goes against the one made in the reading that acid rain is mainly produced by sulfur dioxide.

Finally, the professor contends that sulfur dioxide is not seriously harmful to one's health. He argues that the people who get sick after being exposed to sulfur dioxide are in at-risk groups, such as infants and the elderly. He goes on to explain that sulfur dioxide rarely makes healthy people sick and that other chemicals, such as carbon monoxide, are much more harmful. This contradicts the reading passage's argument that sulfur dioxide creates many health problems.

Critical Analysis Refer to the sample response to complete the tasks below.

1 Underline the topic sentence in each paragraph.

2 Double underline the sentences that refer to the listening.

3 List some of the transitions the writer uses on the lines below.

_____

_____

Revising Use the guided sample response to help you revise your own response on the previous page. Be sure to incorporate specific vocabulary and phrasing from the guided sample response.

With the sulfur dioxide there are many factories involved. In the one hand it can be consequence however; it also has problems that are not as much apperent. The reading and lecture talk about some of this arugment.

In the article, there are many consequence of sulfur dioxide. First of all, it makes the smog. This is major problem with big cities because, people can't see the trafic. Next of all, is the acid rain. This many fall to earth as sulfur acid and destroy the bulding mostly, in industrial nations. Lastly, it is about the health consequence. You see, sulfur dioxide makes people asthma because it is a chemistry.

On the contrery, in the lecutre it make argument that sulfur dioxide is not allways bad. It's erosal may create the global warming but, it can make it colder also. Secondly, Secondly, sulfer dioxide can not make the acid rain because its not to much, unlike nitragen dioxide. Moreover, the health issues that sulfur dioxide make is not so serious. It say the healty people only get some times sick.

Evaluation Grade the response by using the grid below. A place to take notes has been provided.

Score	5	4	3	2	1	Notes
Development				V		
Organization						
Unity						
Language Use						

Final Score: _____

Critical Analysis Which of the following arguments does the response misrepresent?

Ⓐ Sulfur dioxide exposure generally only affects at-risk groups.

Ⓑ The smog created by sulfur dioxide can greatly reduce visibility.

Ⓒ Acid rain is primarily comprised of chemicals other than sulfur dioxide.

Higher Education Is Only for Good Students

 Q Do you agree or disagree with the following statement? Higher education should only be available to good students. Use specific reasons and examples to support your answer.

◈ **Generating Ideas** The following questions will help you write your response. Answer each with one or two sentences. Plan an answer for both options. Some ideas have been provided to help you.

> ### 💡 Idea Box
> **1** Why do colleges and universities not admit all applicants?
> **2** How can limiting higher education only to good students affect the learning environment?
> **3** In what ways can good students take better advantage of higher education?

▷ **Agree**

Reason 1:

Reason 2:

Reason 3:

> ### 💡 Idea Box
> **1** How can weaker students more greatly benefit from higher education?
> **2** How does opening higher education to more people benefit society?
> **3** In what ways would non-academic areas suffer if higher education were only available to good students?

▷ **Disagree**

Reason 1:

Reason 2:

Reason 3:

◈ **Developing Ideas** Having examined the two options, which do you feel more comfortable developing into an essay?

◈ Planning Use the outline to plan your response to the following: Do you agree or disagree with the following statement? Higher education should only be available to good students. Use specific reasons and examples to support your answer.

Thesis Statement (Agree / Disagree) ....

....

First Supporting Idea ....

....

Supporting Example ....

....

Second Supporting Idea ....

....

Supporting Example ....

....

Third Supporting Idea ....

....

Supporting Example ....

....

Conclusion ....

....

Scaffolding Here are some useful phrases to help you when you write.

Therefore, I agree/disagree with the statement that…

One of the strongest arguments in favor of/ against… is…

To give you an idea, consider the case of…

Diligent students more greatly benefit from higher education because…

Allowing weaker students to obtain a higher education allows them to…

For the reasons illustrated above, it is clear that…

Writing Guide

Do you agree or disagree with the following statement? Higher education should only be available to good students. Use specific reasons and examples to support your answer.

▸ **First Paragraph**

State and discuss thesis

▸ **Second Paragraph**

First main supporting idea

Supporting detail

Example

▸ **Third Paragraph**

Second main supporting idea

Supporting detail

Example

▸ **Fourth Paragraph**

Third main supporting idea

Supporting detail

Example

▸ **Fifth Paragraph**

Conclusion

Read the response carefully to see what makes a response strong.

Vocabulary   Take a few moments to review the vocabulary items that will appear in this response.

bright *adj* intelligent; clever
Only **bright** students are able to take AP classes at my high school.

post-secondary institution *n* a school beyond high school, usually a college or a university
Some examples of **post-secondary institutions** are colleges, universities, and technical schools.

community college *n* a college that grants two-year degrees and does not offer housing
I am working toward my associate degree in accounting at the local **community college**.

vocational school *n* a school that teaches skilled trades such as carpentry, construction, and plumbing
My older brother went to a **vocational school** and now makes a lot of money as a carpenter.

keen *adj* eager and enthusiastic
He was **keen** to go on the vacation that he had been planning.

matriculate *v* to enroll as student
Because of her high grades, strong SAT score, and keen personality, Sandy was able to **matriculate** into Harvard.

prestigious *adj* widely known and respected
Oxford University is the most **prestigious** post-secondary institution in the U.K.

elite *n* the part or group having the highest quality, importance, or power
Ivy League universities are reserved for the academic **elite**.

myriad *n* any very large number
Although female soldiers were once a rarity, there are now a **myriad** of women serving in the armed forces.

Traditionally, higher education was reserved only for bright, academically inclined students. This is no longer the case. Today, there are several different types of post-secondary institutions that help students from all backgrounds develop the academic and technical skills needed for success in the professional world. Therefore, I disagree with the statement that only good students should have access to higher education.

One of the strongest arguments in favor of allowing more students to have access to higher education is the many different types of schools that exist. In the past, higher education consisted exclusively of college and universities. But during the twentieth century, new types of higher education institutions, such as community colleges and vocational schools, were developed with the aim of preparing students for the workforce rather than a career in academics. Today, students with weaker academic backgrounds but who have a keen interest in a specific professional field can receive a higher education at a vocational school.

Allowing weaker students to obtain a higher education also enables them to grow academically. To give you an idea, consider the case of one of my close friends, who had poor grades in high school but nevertheless wanted to attend college. Although universities denied him entry, he was able to matriculate into a community college. There, he developed an interest in history and began taking his studies seriously. His grades improved dramatically, and after two years, he was able to transfer to a four-year university. Today, he is getting his master's degree at one of the most prestigious universities in the country. For my friend and many others like him, higher education provided a way for self-improvement.

In conclusion, although higher education was reserved only for the intellectual elite, today its purpose has expanded to educating students from a myriad of academic backgrounds. For the reasons illustrated above, it is clear that higher education should be available to all students.

Critical Analysis Refer to the sample response to complete the tasks below.

1 Underline the topic sentence in each paragraph.

2 Double underline the sentences that include supporting details.

3 List some of the examples the writer uses on the lines below.

_____

_____

Revising Use the guided sample response to help you revise your own response to the question. Be sure to incorporate specific vocabulary and phrasing from the guided sample response.

Attend college is very important to most peolpe. However, the college most be carefull about who they edmit to their program. This is why I believe that only good student should attend secondary school.

First of all, good schools want good student. This because the good studnet more like work hard. In order to obtan the success, as student must very dillengently. For example consider the Ivy Leauge schools. Those schools only want the best and the brightest. This is because their reputuation is very high. They only wanting the student who make the high grades. So only good student are allowed to those colleges.

Also, the students who are allready good can do more better. That because they are able to working hard at the schoolwork. Like my brother was student he worked so hard. And because this he go to a great univercity. Like the good students, my brother take advantige his secondary school education. And there he had much successful. So this supports my reason.

For some studies, students should only be good. Like consider lawer, doctor, etc. They need to have good students to study those subject. In other words, some subject only good students can study. For example, if the doctor graduate for college but he did not study good, how is he a good doctor? You must be sure about quality of your doctor, so the good student only can be taken. Same with the lawer. If the lawer have graduate from good school, he must be very good. That want you can trust.

In conclusion, secondary schools must only consideration of good students. Although bad students can also recieve benefets at college, good student can relieve more from college. For this reason why only good student should attend secondary school.

Evaluation Grade the response by using the grid below. A place to take notes has been provided.

Score	5	4	3	2	1	Notes
Development						
Organization						
Unity			V			
Language Use						

Final Score: _____

Critical Analysis Which of the following arguments could be added to strengthen the response?

Ⓐ Student diversity can improve a school's academic environment.

Ⓑ More diligent students are better able to take advantage of a higher education.

Ⓒ Some jobs requiring a college degree include teacher, accountant, and engineer.

Chapter 11

Integrated Writing
◊ Zoology: The Purpose of Zebra Stripes

Independent Writing
◊ Art Galleries and Musical Performances vs. Sports Facilities

Zoology: The Purpose of Zebra Stripes

Vocabulary　Take a few moments to review the vocabulary items that will appear in this task.

animal kingdom *n*　a classification of living organisms that includes all living animals

Zebras, lions, and human beings are all part of the **animal kingdom**.

herd *n*　a number of cattle or other large animals feeding or living together

The sheepdog protects the **herd** from wolf attacks.

predator *n*　a living creature that feeds on other living creatures

Human beings are one of the only animals with no natural **predators**.

optical illusion *n*　an image that is perceived to be different than it actually is

An **optical illusion** makes something appear different than it really is.

leap *v*　a light, self-propelled movement upward or forward

As the famous saying goes, it is best to look before you **leap**.

prematurely *adv*　too early; too soon

My daughter has many health problems because she was born **prematurely**.

disoriented *adj*　unable to find the correct way or place to go

After coming out of the subway, I became completely **disoriented**.

seamlessly *adv*　perfectly consistent and smooth

One of my favorite things about the movie was how the plot flowed **seamlessly**.

colorblind *adj*　partially or totally unable to tell colors apart from each other

A **colorblind** person might not be able to tell a red traffic light apart from a green one.

distinguish *v*　to notice as being different or unique

Even the twins' mother could not **distinguish** one from the other.

Reading　Read the passage carefully. Be sure to take notes in the margins about the main ideas and the supporting examples from each of the body paragraphs. You have 3 minutes to read.

Perhaps one of the most recognized members of the animal kingdom is the zebra. Much like its relatives, the horse and the donkey, the zebra is a social creature, often traveling in large herds across the African plains. What makes the zebra unique are the black and white stripes covering its entire body. It is this distinctive coloration that protects the zebra from lions, cheetahs, and other predators.

One major purpose of the zebra's stripes is to create an optical illusion. The contrasting black and white stripes on the zebra's body make the animal appear larger than it really is. As a result, predators are tricked into attacking when they are not in a position to do so. Because predators leap at them prematurely, zebras are alerted to their attacker's presence and are thus able to escape the failed attack.

Moreover, the zebra's stripes serve to confuse predators. The repeating pattern of black and white stripes gives a herd of zebras the appearance of being one large animal. This makes it nearly impossible for a predator to identify an individual out of a herd. When threatened, the herd will flee, appearing to the hunter as a confused mass of black and white stripes.

📖 **Margin Notes**

The disoriented predator is unable to focus on one individual and is therefore likely to fail the hunt.

Another important function of the zebra's stripes is camouflage. The black and white stripes help the zebra blend seamlessly into its surroundings. This is possible because the zebra's chief predators are colorblind and unable to distinguish between the zebra and the surrounding environment. Zebras' stripes therefore allow them to hide in tall grass to avoid predators.

Glossary **plain** *n* a large, flat, usually treeless area of land

◊ **Note-Taking** Refer to the reading to complete the outline below.

1 Main Idea of the Passage:

2 First Supporting Argument:

3 Second Supporting Argument:

4 Third Supporting Argument:

(**Critical Thinking**) Consider the following questions. Answer them in complete sentences.

1 Zebras are very fast runners. How does this fact potentially weaken the arguments in the passage?

2 What purposes other than those mentioned in the passage might zebras' stripes serve?

ineffectual *adj* not having produced the proper or intended effect; useless

Our strongest weapons were **ineffectual** against the alien.

imminent *adj* expected to happen soon

As the bombers flew overhead, I knew an attack was **imminent**.

prey *n* an animal hunted and killed for food

This year saw fifty-nine tigers fall **prey** to hunters who killed them for their skins.

go [in] for the kill *exp* to prepare to defeat someone completely when that person is already in a weak position

Wait until your opponent is weakened before you **go in for the kill**.

be thrown off *phr v* to become confused; not to be able to follow

The detective **was thrown off** the killer's trail when he was no longer able to find any new clues.

mono-colored *adj* having only one color

Bulls are **mono-colored** animals while cows are usually multicolored.

confound *v* to cause to become confused or puzzled

The patient's sudden recovery **confounded** doctors.

in plain sight *exp* to be out in the open

The suspect was able to avoid capture by hiding **in plain sight**.

potential *adj* capable of being but not yet existing

The plan has been delayed due to **potential** problems with the funding.

preemptive *adj* designed or having the power to prevent an expected situation or occurrence

To prevent serious destruction from occurring, we must launch a **preemptive** strike against our enemy.

♦ **Listening** Now listen to part of a lecture on the topic you just read about.

02-11

◈ **Note-Taking** Refer to the listening to complete the outline below.

1 Main Idea of the Lecture:

....

....

2 First Supporting Argument:

....

....

3 Second Supporting Argument:

....

....

4 Third Supporting Argument:

....

....

(**Critical Thinking**) Consider the following questions. Answer them in complete sentences.

1 In what ways does the professor refute the points made in the reading?

2 What examples does the professor provide to support her arguments?

◆ **Tandem Note-Taking** Refer to the outlines for the reading and the listening to complete the side-by-side notes below. Include only the three points from the reading and the listening that clearly contradict each other.

Reading	Listening
Main Idea	**Main Idea**
First Supporting Argument	**First Supporting Argument**
Supporting Detail	Supporting Detail
Second Supporting Argument	**Second Supporting Argument**
Supporting Detail	Supporting Detail
Third Supporting Argument	**Third Supporting Argument**
Supporting Detail	Supporting Detail

Scaffolding Here are some useful phrases to help you when you write.

The passage and the lecture both discuss…

In the lecture, it is argued that… This contradicts the reading passage's claim that…

The professor begins by stating that…

This refutes the passage's claim that…

Next, the instructor mentions that…

This is supported by the findings of zoologists, who found that…

The lecturer notes that… and concludes that…

This calls into question the idea that … as was suggested in the reading passage.

◆ **Writing** Use this page to write your response. You have 20 minutes to complete your essay.

Writing Guide	Summarize the points made in the lecture, being sure to explain how they challenge specific arguments made in the reading passage.

▸ **First Paragraph**

State and discuss thesis

▸ **Second Paragraph**

First main idea from lecture

Supporting detail

Contradiction from reading

▸ **Third Paragraph**

Second main idea from lecture

Supporting detail

Contradiction from reading

▸ **Fourth Paragraph**

Third main idea from lecture

Supporting detail

Contradiction from reading

▸ **Fifth Paragraph**

Conclusion (optional)

The passage and the lecture both discuss the purpose of the zebra's stripes. In the lecture, it is argued that the zebra's stripes do not serve a clear purpose. This contradicts the passage's claim that the stripes protect the zebra from predators.

The professor begins by stating that stripes do not warn the zebra of predator attacks. She explains that the reason is that most of the zebra's predators do not use the leaping method to attack but instead chase the zebra across plains. This refutes the argument made in the reading passage that the stripes create an optical illusion that causes predators to attack prematurely.

Next, the lecturer mentions that the stripes do not confuse predators. This is supported by the findings of zoologists, who found that lions were rarely confused by the zebra's stripes. Moreover, the zoologists discovered that lions were equally capable of hunting both zebras and mono-colored animals. This contradicts the reading passage's claim that the zebra's stripes confuse predators.

Finally, the instructor explains that zebras generally do not hide. The reason is that zebras usually stay in open plains where they can spot predators from far away. This calls into question the idea that the zebra relies on its stripes as camouflage to avoid predators as was suggested in the reading passage.

Critical Analysis Refer to the sample response to complete the tasks below.

1 Underline the topic sentence in each paragraph.

2 Double underline the sentences that refer to the listening.

3 List some of the transitions the writer uses on the lines below.

_____

_____

Revising Use the guided sample response to help you revise your own response on the previous page. Be sure to incorporate specific vocabulary and phrasing from the guided sample response.

The lectuer present an option different then the reading passage. That said the strips are protect from the prediters. This is what most people think of the zebra strips.

However, the listening said other wise.

Firstly, the zebra does not attacked by being leap. So their strips is not efficitve as stopping the attack. Usually, the attack is across a plane, until the zebra has fatigue. But the reading passages it was said different.

Secondly, the zebra strips are'nt that confusing. What this means is that the preditors can tell the zebras from another. It also said the lions hunt the monocolor animals as well. This is unlike the article.

Thirdly, the zebra like to stay in open planes and the strips do not assist because of the plane sight. This means that the zebra easily sees prediters themselves. However, also the prediter can see them, so it can be made dangerous. Like was said before, the stripes assit to hide the zebra in the grass.

Evaluation Grade the response by using the grid below. A place to take notes has been provided.

Score	5	4	3	2	1	Notes
Development						
Organization						
Unity				V		
Language Use						

Final Score: _____

Critical Analysis Which body paragraph does not connect the points between the reading passage and the lecture?

(A) Body paragraph 1
(B) Body paragraph 2
(C) Body paragraph 3

Art Galleries and Musical Performances vs. Sports Facilities

 Q Do you agree or disagree with the following statement? The government should spend money to support art galleries and musical performances rather than sports facilities. Use specific reasons and examples to support your answer.

◈ **Generating Ideas** The following questions will help you write your response. Answer each with one or two sentences. Plan an answer for both options. Some ideas have been provided to help you.

> 💡 **Idea Box**
>
> **1** How are art and music related to culture?
> **2** How can people benefit if they government supports art and music?
> **3** Where do people go to see art and music?

▷ **Agree**

Reason 1:

Reason 2:

Reason 3:

> 💡 **Idea Box**
>
> **1** What role do sports have in people's lives?
> **2** Why should the government support people who want to play sports?
> **3** What benefits do sports provide for people?

▷ **Disagree**

Reason 1:

Reason 2:

Reason 3:

◈ **Developing Ideas** Having examined the two options, which do you feel more comfortable developing into an essay?

◆ **Planning** Use the outline to plan your response to the following: Do you agree or disagree with the following statement? The government should spend money to support art galleries and musical performances rather than sports facilities. Use specific reasons and examples to support your answer.

Thesis Statement (Agree / Disagree) ....

....

First Supporting Idea ....

....

Supporting Example ....

....

Second Supporting Idea ....

....

Supporting Example ....

....

Third Supporting Idea ....

....

Supporting Example ....

....

Conclusion ....

....

Scaffolding Here are some useful phrases to help you when you write.

I strongly agree with the statement.

For starters, art galleries and musical performances…

The government needs to support… so that people can…

A second reason is that it is…

The government needs to…

Finally, there are plenty of places in my city for people to…

The government should clearly prioritize…

◈ Writing Use this page to write your response. You have 30 minutes to complete your essay.

Writing Guide

Do you agree or disagree with the following statement? The government should spend money to support art galleries and musical performances rather than sports facilities. Use specific reasons and examples to support your answer.

▸ **First Paragraph**

State and discuss thesis

▸ **Second Paragraph**

First main supporting idea

Supporting detail

Example

▸ **Third Paragraph**

Second main supporting idea

Supporting detail

Example

▸ **Fourth Paragraph**

Third main supporting idea

Supporting detail

Example

▸ **Fifth Paragraph**

Conclusion

Vocabulary Take a few moments to review the vocabulary items that will appear in this response.

aspect *n* the nature, quality, or character of something
He discussed the **aspect** of the project that interested him the most.

tradition *n* something that is handed down from generation to generation
It is important to remember the **traditions** of your culture.

lesson *n* a section that a course is divided into
She always has a piano **lesson** after school on Friday afternoon.

step in *phr v* to involve oneself in a certain matter
The teacher had to **step in** and stop the two students from arguing with each other.

experience *v* to participate in a certain activity
It would be wonderful to have a chance to **experience** a day in outer space.

display *v* to show something, such as at a museum or gallery
The museum **displays** many dinosaur fossils that were found in the local area.

funds *n* money that is available and can be spent
They have enough **funds** to pay for a trip to Hawaii this summer.

prioritize *v* to put something ahead of another thing in order of importance
You must **prioritize** your duties and complete the most important work first.

I strongly agree with the statement. In my opinion, the government should definitely spend money to support art galleries and musical performances rather than spend money to support sports facilities. I feel this way for a few reasons. Let me explain my thoughts on this matter now.

For starters, art galleries and musical performances are an important aspect of culture. In my country, we have many famous artists. We also have a musical tradition that goes back hundreds of years. The government needs to support art galleries so that people can visit these facilities to see artwork that is produced by artists in my country. It should also support musical performances for the same reason. People need to be able to learn about important aspects of their own culture.

A second reason is that it is not easy for people to become artists or musicians. They have to spend a great amount of money on lessons when they are young. In addition, musical instruments can cost thousands of dollars. My brother was in his school band, and it cost my parents very much money to buy him a trumpet. When people finally become artists or musicians, they do not make much money as well. So they often lead difficult lives. The government needs to step in and help these artists and musicians.

Finally, there are plenty of places in my city for people to watch sporting events, yet there are few places for them to experience the arts. I believe this is wrong. The government needs to spend money to construct galleries for displaying art. It should spend money to build concert halls where people can see musical performances. This would be a great use of taxpayer funds.

The government should clearly prioritize art galleries and musical performances over sporting events. Art and music are important to a country's culture, it is hard for people to become artists or musicians, and there are already very many places to see sporting events. Government funds need to be spent on art and music.

Critical Analysis Refer to the sample response to complete the tasks below.

1 Underline the topic sentence in each paragraph.

2 Double underline the sentences that include supporting details.

3 List some of the examples the writer uses on the lines below.

_____

_____

Revising Use the guided sample response to help you revise your own response to the question. Be sure to incorporate specific vocabulary and phrasing from the guided sample response.

I am disagree with statement. I like sports more than art and music. So I want government to make sports facilities.

First, sports are fun to watch. Me and my friends love to see sports. We watch basketball and football on the TV. But we can't go to games. Why not? There is no stadiums in city. Government needs make stadiums for the people. Then, the people will happy. Me and my friends happy also.

Two, many people are the fat. So they not healthy. If people play sports, they not be fat. They be healthy. My brother was fat. He always played computer. Then he played soccer. He wasnot fat. He got okay. More people can be like him. They just need place to play sports. If no have, cannot lose fat. If have, can become person in the good shape.

Three, art and music are boring. Sports are fun. People need more fun in their life. Let's make places to have fun. Then people be happy. I don't want unhappy in life. I don't want look at art. I don't want listen music. I just want play. Play sports will be fun.

I don't want government to spend money on art and music. That is waste of money. Government needs to give sports to people. Then people will be happy and not fat.

Evaluation Grade the response by using the grid below. A place to take notes has been provided.

Score	5	4	3	2	1	Notes
Development						
Organization		V				
Unity						
Language Use						

Final Score: _____

Critical Analysis Which of the following arguments could be added to strengthen the response?

Ⓐ A new stadium in my city would make so many people very happy.

Ⓑ People would love to have a new health center to make sure they do not get sick.

Ⓒ It would be okay for the government to spend some money on art and music.

Part

B

Chapter 12

Integrated Writing
◈ Psychology: TV Addiction

Independent Writing
◈ Traveling Is Better with a Tour Guide

Psychology: TV Addiction

Vocabulary Take a few moments to review the vocabulary items that will appear in this task.

overindulgence *n* the act of satisfying a desire or habit to excess

Overindulgence is nearly always unhealthy.

phenomenon *n* any state or process known through the senses rather than by intuition or reasoning

Hurricanes, earthquakes, and tidal waves are all natural **phenomena**.

manifest *v* to reveal a presence or to make an appearance

The main character's true intentions did not **manifest** themselves until the end of the book.

involuntary *adj* acting or done without or against one's will

Some of your body's **involuntary** actions include blinking and breathing.

anxiety *n* a feeling of great uneasiness or concern

I always feel **anxiety** before giving a speech in front of a large group of people.

merely *adv* nothing more than that; only

This is not a serious problem but **merely** an inconvenience.

indulge *v* to yield to; to satisfy a craving

Feel free to **indulge** yourself in our selection of fine wines and cheeses from around the world.

conflict *v* to be in or come into opposition; to differ

We can never agree about anything because her opinions always **conflict** with mine.

interpersonal *adj* of or relating to the interactions between individuals

Managers must have good **interpersonal** skills.

Reading Read the passage carefully. Be sure to take notes in the margins about the main ideas and the supporting examples from each of the body paragraphs. You have 3 minutes to read.

For many people, watching television can be a relaxing and enjoyable way to spend time. However, as with all pleasurable activities, there is the potential danger of overindulgence. Television addiction is a well-documented phenomenon that has numerous serious side effects.

The problems associated with television watching manifest themselves after prolonged viewing. People who watch television twenty-eight hours or more per week show symptoms similar to those of patients suffering from clinical gambling addiction. Heavy watchers claim that their viewing is involuntary and find it difficult to replace television watching with more productive activities in spite of being aware of the damage their viewing behavior causes to their lives. For these people, watching television is a self-perpetuating habit that cannot be easily broken.

Studies have also shown that heavy watchers suffer from emotional problems. Psychologists have found that these people turn to television in order to alleviate feelings of loneliness and anxiety. However, watching television does not act as a substitute for real-life experiences but merely serves as a temporary distraction from these negative emotions. Whenever the television is taken away, heavy viewers suffer from withdrawal symptoms, including nervousness and irritation, and they often describe feelings of discomfort and boredom.

Television addiction affects not only the viewer but also that person's

📖 **Margin Notes**

friends and family members. People around those who indulge in excessive amounts of television viewing describe these people as addicts. These claims are supported by research, which shows that heavy viewers are generally physically and emotionally withdrawn and much less likely to participate in social activities. They often arrange their personal schedules so that they do not conflict with their viewing schedule. As expected, this extreme devotion to television often damages real-world interpersonal relationships.

Glossary　**clinical**　*adj*　involving or based on the direct observation of patients
　　　withdrawal symptom　*n*　a physical or emotioual problem that occurs when an addict stops using the substance to which that person is addicted

◆ **Note-Taking**　Refer to the reading to complete the outline below.

1　Main Idea of the Passage:

2　First Supporting Argument:

3　Second Supporting Argument:

4　Third Supporting Argument:

(Critical Thinking)　Consider the following questions. Answer them in complete sentences.

1　How are the symptoms caused by heavy viewing similar to those caused by other activities?

2　What is flawed about the argument presented in the second body paragraph?

Vocabulary Take a few moments to review the vocabulary items that will appear in this task.

hold water *exp* to stand up to critical examination
I am sorry, but your arguments simply do not **hold water**.

unwind *v* to become free of nervous tension; to relax
My father always liked to **unwind** before dinner by having a glass of wine.

passive *adj* not active; acted upon
His **passive** attitude made it easy to influence his opinion.

crave *v* to have an intense desire for
Whenever I travel, I always **crave** my mother's cooking.

establish *v* to prove the truth of
The attorneys were able to **establish** the innocence of their client.

correlation *n* a logical or natural association between two or more things
Just because there is a **correlation** between winter weather and getting a cold does not mean that one causes the other.

jury is still out *exp* a decision has not been reached on someone or something
The **jury is still out** on the question of building a new student dormitory.

address *v* to deliver a speech
The president failed to **address** the financial crisis in his speech this afternoon.

narrow *adj* limited in scope or understanding
In ancient times, people had a **narrow** view of the world.

consensus *n* an opinion or position reached by a group as a whole
By the 1960s, doctors had reached a **consensus** that smoking causes cancer.

◊ **Listening** Now listen to part of a lecture on the topic you just read about.

02-12

◈ **Note-Taking** Refer to the listening to complete the outline below.

1 Main Idea of the Lecture:

2 First Supporting Argument:

3 Second Supporting Argument:

4 Third Supporting Argument:

(Critical Thinking) Consider the following questions. Answer them in complete sentences.

1 In what ways does the instructor refute the points made in the reading?

2 In what ways does the instructor fail to address the arguments made in the reading?

◈ **Tandem Note-Taking** Refer to the outlines for the reading and the listening to complete the side-by-side notes below. Include only the three points from the reading and the listening that clearly contradict each other.

Reading

Main Idea

....

....

First Supporting Argument

....

....

Supporting Detail

....

....

Second Supporting Argument

....

....

Supporting Detail

....

....

Third Supporting Argument

....

....

Supporting Detail

....

....

Listening

Main Idea

....

....

First Supporting Argument

....

....

Supporting Detail

....

....

Second Supporting Argument

....

....

Supporting Detail

....

....

Third Supporting Argument

....

....

Supporting Detail

....

....

Scaffolding   Here are some useful phrases to help you when you write.

The reading passage and the lecture both deal with…

The lecturer casts doubt on the idea of… therefore going against the arguments presented in…

First, the professor states that…

This challenges the reading's assertion that…

Furthermore, the instructor says that…

These arguments contradict those in the reading passage, which contends…

Finally, the lecturer discusses…

This calls into question the arguments presented in the reading passage that…

Writing Guide	Summarize the points made in the lecture, being sure to explain how they cast doubt on specific claims made in the reading passage.

▸ **First Paragraph**

State and discuss thesis

▸ **Second Paragraph**

First main idea from lecture

Supporting detail

Contradiction from reading

▸ **Third Paragraph**

Second main idea from lecture

Supporting detail

Contradiction from reading

▸ **Fourth Paragraph**

Third main idea from lecture

Supporting detail

Contradiction from reading

▸ **Fifth Paragraph**

Conclusion (optional)

The reading passage and the lecture both deal with the issue of television addiction. The lecturer casts doubt on the idea of television addiction. Her arguments go against the ones presented in the reading passage.

First, the professor states that watching television is a good way to relax during your free time. Because watching television is a passive activity, your body and mind are able to rest. Furthermore, watching television can reduce stress because it lowers your heart rate. These points refute the reading passage's claim that watching television leads to addiction symptoms that disrupt people's lives.

Next, the instructor explains that people naturally feel anxious and lonely whenever something they crave is not around, be it television or family and friends. Additionally, researchers have yet to establish a correlation between television watching and depression. These arguments contradict those in the reading passage, which contends that people turn to television in order to alleviate feelings of loneliness and anxiety.

Finally, the lecturer delves into the confusion over the word addiction. For the general public, the word addiction has a broad meaning while for psychologists, it has a narrow clinical meaning. The professor also mentions that psychologists have yet to reach a consensus about whether prolonged television viewing has serious consequences. This calls into question the reading passage's argument that all heavy viewers are emotionally withdrawn addicts.

Critical Analysis Refer to the sample response to complete the tasks below.

1 Underline the topic sentence in each paragraph.

2 Double underline the sentences that refer to the listening.

3 List some of the transitions the writer uses on the lines below.

_____

_____

Revising Use the guided sample response to help you revise your own response on the previous page. Be sure to incorporate specific vocabulary and phrasing from the guided sample response.

The listening and the reading both talk about television addiction. While the reading says that television addiction has numerous side effects the listening goes against this.

First of all, the reading says that people who watch more than 28 hours of tv each week have addiction symptoms similar than gambling addiction and heavy watchers have hard times being productive. However the listening refutes this saying that television has many benefits, like getting rest and reducing stress.

Next, the listening talked about the negative emotions that television causes. It said that missing television causes negative emotions, and this is unlike the reading, where it said heavy television viewing creates feelings of loneleness and anxiety. It also said that viewers suffer withdrawl symptoms when the tv is not around.

Finally, the lectuer mentions that people are confused about the word addiction. She said that most people think addiction is something you enjoy, however pyschologists only use the word in a clinical meaning. The reading, on the other hand, explains that people who watch a lot of tv are addicted and have lots of problems. Though the listening differs again and illustrates that there is no clear idea of whether tv addiction is for real.

In conclusion, the reading argues that tv addiction is a serious problem, however the reasons given in the lecture above show that this might not be the truth.

Evaluation Grade the response by using the grid below. A place to take notes has been provided.

Score	5	4	3	2	1	Notes
Development						
Organization						
Unity						
Language Use	V					

Final Score: _____

Critical Analysis Which of the main body paragraphs does not develop the points made in the lecture?

- Ⓐ Body paragraph 1
- Ⓑ Body paragraph 2
- Ⓒ Body paragraph 3

Traveling Is Better with a Tour Guide

 Q Do you agree or disagree with the following statement? It is better to travel in a group with a tour guide than to travel alone. Give specific reasons and examples to support your answer.

◈**Generating Ideas** The following questions will help you write your response. Answer each with one or two sentences. Plan an answer for both options. Some ideas have been provided to help you.

> **💡 Idea Box**
>
> 1 How can traveling in a group be more efficient than traveling alone?
> 2 How can traveling with a tour guide be safer?
> 3 In what ways can traveling with a tour group led by a tour guide be more interesting?

▷ **Agree**

Reason 1:

Reason 2:

Reason 3:

> **💡 Idea Box**
>
> 1 How can traveling in a tour group be a more limiting experience?
> 2 How does traveling with a tour guide lessen the sense of adventure?
> 3 How can traveling as part of a tour group be less relaxing than traveling by yourself?

▷ **Disagree**

Reason 1:

Reason 2:

Reason 3:

◈**Developing Ideas** Having examined the two options, which do you feel more comfortable developing into an essay?

◈ Planning Use the outline to plan your response to the following: Do you agree or disagree with the following statement? It is better to travel in a group with a tour guide than to travel alone. Give specific reasons and examples to support your answer.

Thesis Statement (Agree / Disagree) ....

....

First Supporting Idea ....

....

Supporting Example ....

....

Second Supporting Idea ....

....

Supporting Example ....

....

Third Supporting Idea ....

....

Supporting Example ....

....

Conclusion ....

....

Scaffolding Here are some useful phrases to help you when you write.

For these reasons, I agree/disagree with the statement that…

For one, traveling in a group allows you to…

Instead of having to wait in line, you can simply…

Tour groups usually only visit tourist hotspots, meaning that…

You never have to worry about… when you are with…

Traveling independently allows you to…

Although… might be better for some people, traveling in tour groups/alone is…

◈ Writing
Use this page to write your response. You have 30 minutes to complete your essay.

Writing Guide	Do you agree or disagree with the following statement? It is better to travel in a group with a tour guide than to travel alone. Give specific reasons and examples to support your answer.

▸ **First Paragraph**

State and discuss
thesis

▸ **Second Paragraph**

First main
supporting idea

Supporting detail

Example

▸ **Third Paragraph**

Second main
supporting idea

Supporting detail

Example

▸ **Fourth Paragraph**

Third main
supporting idea

Supporting detail

Example

▸ **Fifth Paragraph**

Conclusion

Vocabulary Take a few moments to review the vocabulary items that will appear in this response.

exotic *adj* from another part of the world; foreign
The greenhouse is home to several **exotic** tropical plants.

itinerary *n* a route or planned route of a journey
The first stop on our **itinerary** is England, and then we will go to France and Germany.

destination *n* a place where a person or thing is being sent
You will be notified via email when your package arrives at its **destination**.

limited *adj* restricted in some way
Knowledge is **limited**. Imagination encircles the world.

firsthand *adj* received from the original source; direct
You should only trust news that you hear **firsthand**.

hassle *n* trouble; annoyance
Going to the post office is one of my least favorite activities because it is such a **hassle**.

Going on vacation is a great opportunity to visit exotic locales and to experience foreign cultures. But it can also be a time-consuming and stressful experience, especially when traveling abroad. For these reasons, I agree with the statement that it is better to travel in a group with a tour guide than to travel alone.

For one, traveling in a group allows you to spend more time enjoying your vacation. The reason is that tour groups follow preplanned itineraries that are designed for both maximum pleasure and efficiency. Such was the case when I visited Hong Kong. Instead of having to wait in line to buy tickets for every attraction I visited, I was able to enter immediately because the tour guide had already purchased tickets for our tour group. I also did not have to worry about transportation because my tour group was taken around the city on our own tour bus. Thanks to my tour guide, I was able to take in most of the sights in Hong Kong even though I was only there for a limited amount of time.

Another benefit of traveling in a tour group is that it makes vacationing safer. As a visitor in a foreign country, there is a greater risk for potential problems to occur. When you travel with tour guides, who are knowledgeable about the local area, language, and customs, you mitigate this risk. This was definitely true when I visited Vietnam. There, I was hiking up a mountain when I tripped on some rocks and broke my ankle. Had I been alone, without a cell phone, not knowing where to seek medical attention, and not speaking Vietnamese, I might have been in serious trouble. However, since I was with a tour guide, I was able to get the help I needed quickly and without any problems.

For adventurous people who want to experience all aspects of a foreign culture firsthand, traveling alone is best. But for most people who want to experience the pleasures of a vacation without all of the hassles, traveling in a group with a tour guide is the superior choice.

Critical Analysis Refer to the sample response to complete the tasks below.

1 Underline the topic sentence in each paragraph.

2 Double underline the sentences that include supporting details.

3 List some of the examples the writer uses on the lines below.

_____

_____

Revising Use the guided sample response to help you revise your own response to the question. Be sure to incorporate specific vocabulary and phrasing from the guided sample response.

travelling can be a lot of fun. it can be hard to. since this many peple think it better to have travel guide to guide them. but i don't think this. so i disagree with the sentence above because you lose adventure, it is less exotic and it isn't too relaxing.

first thing is you lose the adventure. your trip is less excitement. there are reason for this. since you don't do things alone you don't know about the local costoms. this means the vacation is less interresting. i think vactions should be alot of excitement, but the tour guide makes it less. but when you go to the place by your self, it can have more adverture.

also travelling with the tour guide is less exotic. this happens because you don't travel any where special. one time i went to veitnam. there i went to many places in the tour group, but these places weren't exotic. they were just the average place in the city. going on the tour group didn't see me anything interesting. like the buildings in that place. so i feel very sorry for that trip. if i travel alone i would have more exotic and exciting trip. these things are too important when you vaction.

thirdly the vocation has more relaxing when travel alone. in order words, when you travel with tour group you don't have the time to rest. this is because of many reason. the tour group must hurry, so you can't relax. also, their schedule. it has to be on time or else the others get angray. my friend want to the vaction also on the tour group. he said they did alot of stuffs and seed many sites. but he could not get relaxed. i thought this way at my vaction. he was so tired after his vaction. he had to come home and take a rest. so for this the alone vaction is better.

at conclusion, i have travel many time. some times it was fun with tour group. most of times it was not too fun. as i explain in this essay going alone to the vacation has the greater benefits.

Evaluation ▸ Grade the response by using the grid below. A place to take notes has been provided.

Score	5	4	3	2	1	Notes
Development						
Organization						
Unity				V		
Language Use						

Final Score: _____

Critical Analysis ▸ Which of the following arguments could be added to strengthen the response?

You rarely have the opportunity to interact with the locals or to learn some of their language.

Ⓐ Body paragraph 1

Ⓑ Body paragraph 2

Ⓒ Body paragraph 3

Part

C

Experiencing the TOEFL iBT Actual Tests

Actual Test 01

Writing Section Directions

03-01

 Make sure your headset is on.

This section measures your ability to use writing to communicate in an academic environment. There will be two writing tasks.

For the first writing task, you will read a passage and listen to a lecture and then answer a question based on what you have read and heard. For the second writing task, you will answer a question based on your own knowledge and experience.

Now listen to the directions for the first writing task.

Task 1

Writing Based on
Reading and Listening

03-02

For this task, you will first have 3 minutes to read a passage about an academic topic. You may take notes on the passage if you wish. The passage will then be removed and you will listen to a lecture about the same topic. While you listen, you may also take notes.

Then you will have **20 minutes** to write a response to a question that asks you about the relationship between the lecture you heard and the reading passage. Try to answer the question as completely as possible using information from the reading passage and the lecture. The question does not ask you to express your personal opinion. You will be able to see the reading passage again when it is time for you to write. You may use your notes to help you answer the question.

Typically, an effective response will be 150 to 225 words long. Your response will be judged on the quality of your writing and on the completeness and accuracy of the content. If you finish your response before time is up, you may click on **Next** to go on to the second writing task.

Now you will see the reading passage for 3 minutes. Remember it will be available to you again while you are writing. Immediately after the reading time ends, the lecture will begin, so keep your headset on until the lecture is over.

People have been using antibiotics for thousands of years, but it was not until the twentieth century that they were really understood. Antibiotics are utilized by doctors to cure patients of a wide variety of bacterial diseases. In the 1900s—and especially from the 1940s to the 1960s—large numbers of antibiotics were discovered. They have been used to treat countless numbers of people and have saved the lives of millions. These people have gone on to recover from their illnesses and live long, happy lives.

One of the primary benefits of antibiotics is that they are highly effective. By taking them orally or topically, sick individuals are able to recover from a wide number of infections and diseases. These include both simple infections as well as complicated ones. Thanks to penicillin and numerous other antibiotics, people no longer have to suffer through periods of painful infections, nor do they die because of relatively basic problems like infected teeth anymore. Instead, people take antibiotics and see their problems vanish rapidly.

Another advantage of antibiotics is that their usage can reduce the number of surgical operations which doctors need to perform. Essentially, by taking prescribed doses of antibiotics, patients can have their medical issues solved. As a result, there is no need for these patients to undergo risky surgical procedures. This too has helped keep vast numbers of patients alive.

A final advantage is that antibiotics are able to prevent diseases from spreading and becoming worse. For instance, individuals with the common cold are likely to develop pneumonia if their colds persist and get worse. However, by taking antibiotics, the severity of their colds can be reduced, and their problems will not develop into something that has the potential to be fatal.

03-03

Directions You have 20 minutes to plan and write your response. Your response will be judged on the basis of the quality of your writing and on how well your response presents the points in the lecture and their relationship to the reading passage. Typically, an effective response will be 150 to 225 words.

Question Summarize the points made in the lecture, being sure to explain how they cast doubt on specific points made in the reading passage.

Copy Cut Paste   Word Count: 0

People have been using antibiotics for thousands of years, but it was not until the twentieth century that they were really understood. Antibiotics are utilized by doctors to cure patients of a wide variety of bacterial diseases. In the 1900s—and especially from the 1940s to the 1960s—large numbers of antibiotics were discovered. They have been used to treat countless numbers of people and have saved the lives of millions. These people have gone on to recover from their illnesses and live long, happy lives.

One of the primary benefits of antibiotics is that they are highly effective. By taking them orally or topically, sick individuals are able to recover from a wide number of infections and diseases. These include both simple infections as well as complicated ones. Thanks to penicillin and numerous other antibiotics, people no longer have to suffer through periods of painful infections, nor do they die because of relatively basic problems like infected teeth anymore. Instead, people take antibiotics and see their problems vanish rapidly.

Another advantage of antibiotics is that their usage can reduce the number of surgical operations which doctors need to perform. Essentially, by taking prescribed doses of antibiotics, patients can have their medical issues solved. As a result, there is no need for these patients to undergo risky surgical procedures. This too has helped keep vast numbers of patients alive.

A final advantage is that antibiotics are able to prevent diseases from spreading and becoming worse. For instance, individuals with the common cold are likely to develop pneumonia if their colds persist and get worse. However, by taking antibiotics, the severity of their colds can be reduced, and their problems will not develop into something that has the potential to be fatal.

Task 2

Writing Based on
Knowledge and Experience

03-04

For this task, you will write an essay in response to a question that asks you to state, explain, and support your opinion on an issue. You will have **30 minutes** to write your essay.

Typically, an effective essay will contain a minimum of 300 words. Your essay will be judged on the quality of your writing. This includes the development of your ideas, the organization of the content, and the quality and accuracy of the language you used to express ideas.

Click on **Continue** to go on.

Copy Cut Paste

Word Count: 0

Directions Read the question below. You have 30 minutes to plan, write, and revise your essay. Typically, an effective response will contain a minimum of 300 words.

Question: Do you agree or disagree with the following statement?

To ensure that you have a good future, it is best to plan carefully while you are still young.

Use specific reasons and examples to support your answer.

Copy Cut Paste

Word Count: 0

Actual Test 02

Writing Section Directions

03-05

 Make sure your headset is on.

This section measures your ability to use writing to communicate in an academic environment. There will be two writing tasks.

For the first writing task, you will read a passage and listen to a lecture and then answer a question based on what you have read and heard. For the second writing task, you will answer a question based on your own knowledge and experience.

Now listen to the directions for the first writing task.

Writing Based on
Reading and Listening

03-06

For this task, you will first have 3 minutes to read a passage about an academic topic. You may take notes on the passage if you wish. The passage will then be removed and you will listen to a lecture about the same topic. While you listen, you may also take notes.

Then you will have **20 minutes** to write a response to a question that asks you about the relationship between the lecture you heard and the reading passage. Try to answer the question as completely as possible using information from the reading passage and the lecture. The question does not ask you to express your personal opinion. You will be able to see the reading passage again when it is time for you to write. You may use your notes to help you answer the question.

Typically, an effective response will be 150 to 225 words long. Your response will be judged on the quality of your writing and on the completeness and accuracy of the content. If you finish your response before time is up, you may click on **Next** to go on to the second writing task.

Now you will see the reading passage for 3 minutes. Remember it will be available to you again while you are writing. Immediately after the reading time ends, the lecture will begin, so keep your headset on until the lecture is over.

The proliferation of the Internet has had a tremendous impact on the way we receive our news. An increasing number of people are abandoning traditional print news sources in favor of online sources. A number of factors make this a change for the better.

One advantage of online news websites is their immediacy. With printed news sources, people receive the news after events have finished. This is not the case with digital news sources. Through online news websites, readers are immediately informed of events as they unfold due to the fact that these websites are updated several times throughout the day. Furthermore, readers are able to access news stories as often as they need to. Because online news websites make their entire database searchable, readers can easily locate any article they wish, regardless of its date of publication.

Another benefit of online news websites is customization. Unlike newspapers and other printed news sources, where readers have to sift through several pages of material they find irrelevant, online news websites allow readers to specify which news stories they want to receive. To do this, readers simply have to create an account and provide some personal background information. In this way, they can read only the articles that are relevant to their interests and concerns.

Lastly, online news sites offer a greater amount of coverage than traditional sources. While printed sources are physically restricted in the amount of news stories they can cover, online news sites do not suffer from this limitation. And because they gather their news from a myriad of sources, online news sites are able to cover stories on a global scale. Thus, readers can easily stay informed about events from around the world at a click of the mouse.

03-07

Directions You have 20 minutes to plan and write your response. Your response will be judged on the basis of the quality of your writing and on how well your response presents the points in the lecture and their relationship to the reading passage. Typically, an effective response will be 150 to 225 words.

Question Summarize the points made in the lecture, being sure to explain how they challenge specific claims made in the reading passage.

Copy Cut Paste   Word Count: 0

The proliferation of the Internet has had a tremendous impact on the way we receive our news. An increasing number of people are abandoning traditional print news sources in favor of online sources. A number of factors make this a change for the better.

One advantage of online news websites is their immediacy. With printed news sources, people receive the news after events have finished. This is not the case with digital news sources. Through online news websites, readers are immediately informed of events as they unfold due to the fact that these websites are updated several times throughout the day. Furthermore, readers are able to access news stories as often as they need to. Because online news websites make their entire database searchable, readers can easily locate any article they wish, regardless of its date of publication.

Another benefit of online news websites is customization. Unlike newspapers and other printed news sources, where readers have to sift through several pages of material they find irrelevant, online news websites allow readers to specify which news stories they want to receive. To do this, readers simply have to create an account and provide some personal background information. In this way, they can read only the articles that are relevant to their interests and concerns.

Lastly, online news sites offer a greater amount of coverage than traditional sources. While printed sources are physically restricted in the amount of news stories they can cover, online news sites do not suffer from this limitation. And because they gather their news from a myriad of sources, online news sites are able to cover stories on a global scale. Thus, readers can easily stay informed about events from around the world at a click of the mouse.

Task 2

Writing Based on
Knowledge and Experience

03-08

For this task, you will write an essay in response to a question that asks you to state, explain, and support your opinion on an issue. You will have **30 minutes** to write your essay.

Typically, an effective essay will contain a minimum of 300 words. Your essay will be judged on the quality of your writing. This includes the development of your ideas, the organization of the content, and the quality and accuracy of the language you used to express ideas.

Click on **Continue** to go on.

Copy Cut Paste   Word Count: 0

Directions Read the question below. You have 30 minutes to plan, write, and revise your essay. Typically, an effective response will contain a minimum of 300 words.

Question: Do you agree or disagree with the following statement?

Life today is easier and more convenient than when your grandparents were children.

Use specific reasons and examples to support your answer.

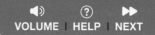
Copy Cut Paste

Word Count: 0

Memo

TOEFL® MAP

MAP Writing

New TOEFL® Edition

Advanced

Scripts and Answer Key

 DARAKWON

TOEFL® MAP Writing

New TOEFL® Edition

Writing

Advanced

Scripts and Answer Key

DARAKWON

Part A
Understanding Writing Question Types

Writing Section

Information Organization Exercise
p.15

Exercise 1

1 Thesis Statement: *Uniforms are a good idea.*

2 First Supporting Argument: *Uniforms are not as expensive as brand-name clothing.*

   Detailed Supporting Example: *One uniform costs little money.*

3 Second Supporting Argument: *Uniforms make it easy to get ready for school.*

   Detailed Supporting Example: *Students do not have to waste time choosing clothing.*

4 Third Supporting Argument: *Uniforms create a sense of unity among students.*

   Detailed Supporting Example: *School colors make students feel like they are a part of a group.*

Exercise 2

1 Thesis Statement: *The nebular hypothesis states that our solar system was formed from a cloud of gas and dust.*

2 First Supporting Argument: *Gravity caused the cloud to flatten and to become disk shaped.*

   Detailed Supporting Example: *Our solar system is shaped like a disk.*

3 Second Supporting Argument: *Solid elements joined together in areas of high gravity.*

   Detailed Supporting Example: *The planets formed in these areas.*

4 Third Supporting Argument: *Most of the nebula's mass became the sun.*

   Detailed Supporting Example: *The sun retains ninety-nine percent of the cloud's mass.*

Introduce 02

Integrated Writing

Note-Taking
p.19

⊘ **Note-Taking Exercise**
   (Answers may vary.)

   1 Main Idea of the Passage: *Schools might be damaging*

their students' academic performance by cutting art and music programs.

2 First Supporting Argument: *Music programs are less expensive to maintain than sports programs.*

3 Second Supporting Argument: *Playing an instrument improves communication between the brainstem and the neocortex.*

4 Third Supporting Argument: *Music education has both intrinsic and extrinsic value.*

Tandem Note-Taking
p.20
(Answers may vary.)

Reading	Listening
Main Idea	**Main Idea**
Music education should not be included in the regular curriculum.	*Schools might be damaging their students' academic performance by cutting art and music programs.*
First Supporting Argument	**First Supporting Argument**
Schools need to attract the best teachers possible.	*Music programs are less expensive to maintain than sports programs.*
Supporting Detail	**Supporting Detail**
need to offer teachers high salaries; cut all programs not included in standardized testing	*students supply instruments; music teachers no high salaries*
Second Supporting Argument	**Second Supporting Argument**
Music education does not improve math and science ability.	*Playing an instrument improves communication between the brainstem and the neocortex.*
Supporting Detail	**Supporting Detail**
music does not rely on logic but rather intuition	*math, science, listening, and foreign language skills improve*
Third Supporting Argument	**Third Supporting Argument**
Music education does not fit in well with our education system.	*Music education has both intrinsic and extrinsic value.*
Supporting Detail	**Supporting Detail**
no definite answers; cannot be graded; should not be graded; expression main pleasure	*music can give career; joy*

Strong Response
p.23

[d] The reading passage and the lecture both address the issue of music education in public schools. [c] The lecture presents arguments in favor of maintaining music programs. Thus it goes against the central argument made

in the reading passage.

[b] First, the lecturer states that music programs are not cost prohibitive. The lecturer mentions that sports programs are far more expensive to maintain than music programs. [e] The reasons are that music students pay for their own equipment and that music teachers are paid much lower salaries than most football coaches. [a] These points contradict the reading passage's argument that music programs are too expensive to maintain.

[b] Next, the lecturer argues that playing an instrument helps improve brain performance. [e] The lecturer goes on to explain that by strengthening the relationship between parts of the brain, students enhance their math and science abilities while improving their listening skills and foreign language learning ability. [a] This goes against the argument made in the reading passage that music does not help students perform better at other subjects.

[b] The lecturer concludes by mentioning that music education has both extrinsic and intrinsic value. That is, it can lead to careers in music for some students while imparting a sense of joy in all music students. [e] Because of this, the lecturer argues, students are able to become happier and more productive in other aspects of their lives. [a] These arguments go a long way in rebutting the reading passage's claim that music education should not be incorporated into the educational system.

Weak Response

p.24

⊘ **Analysis Exercise**

(Answers may vary.)

Score	5	4	3	2	1
Development				V	
Organization			V		
Unity			V		
Language Use			V		

Notes

This response is at level 3. It addresses the main points of the lecture but only mentions one of the points from the reading. More problematic, though, is the lack of development. The final paragraph in particular does not explain the points brought up; rather, it briefly mentions some of the key words from the listening (intrinsic and extrinsic) and simply notes that music is good for schools. This, coupled with consistent minor grammatical mistakes (repeated misuse of "there" for their and "waist" for waste as well as a lack of transitions), keeps the essay from scoring higher.

Final Score: ___3___

Independent Writing

Generating Ideas

p.27

(Answers may vary.)

▷ **Agree**

Reason 1: *By being polite, you can help strengthen your relationships with family and friends.*

Reason 2: *They will likely be kinder and more polite to you.*

Reason 3: *If you are polite to somebody who is in a bad mood, you can make that person feel better.*

▷ **Disagree**

Reason 1: *When you are angry or upset, it might be difficult to remain polite.*

Reason 2: *Generally, you treat strangers with less care because you do not know them and probably will not see them again.*

Reason 3: *When somebody is being rude to you or is not listening to you, it can be better not to be polite.*

Planning

p.28

(Answers may vary.)

Thesis Statement (Agree / Disagree)

I agree with the idea that it is important to be polite and courteous to everyone, even strangers.

First Supporting Idea

Being polite to family members can directly impact your quality of life.

Supporting Example

You spend a lot of time with your family, so you should be nice to them.

Second Supporting Idea

Being polite to strangers can both directly impact your life and indirectly impact all of society.

Supporting Example

By being polite to strangers, you inspire them to be polite to others.

Conclusion

Instead of making the world a more hostile place by being rude, make it a more hospitable place by being courteous.

Strong Response

p.31

[b] The world is becoming a ruder place. Children do not respect their elders. People do not hold doors open for others walking behind them. Customers use bad language

when they do not get the service they want. [d] In this world, where good manner and politeness are becoming increasingly scarce, I agree with the idea that it is important to be polite and courteous to everyone, even strangers.

[f] Being polite to family members can directly impact your quality of life. [c] You are around your family in your most private moments throughout your entire life. Therefore, you need to foster good relationships with your family members. [a] Being rude to your family members simply because you have had a bad day at work does not facilitate harmony and can actually irritate them. But by using such basic courtesies such as "Please" and "Thank you" in the home, you can help members of your family grow closer to one another and help them feel relaxed and comfortable.

[f] Being polite to strangers can both directly impact your life and indirectly impact all of society. [c] Doing something as simple as holding a door open for a stranger can make that person feel less stressed while making yourself feel good. [e] Indeed, research suggests that people living in polite societies tend to be happier. And by being courteous to others, you can influence them to be courteous as well. This will create a domino effect that will permeate throughout the whole of society, which will, in turn, improve the quality of life for everyone.

[a] So the next time you decide against thanking your server at a restaurant, keep this thought in mind: Rudeness is a contagious disease. [g] Instead of making the world a more hostile place by being rude, make it a more hospitable place by being courteous.

Weak Response

p.32

✓ Analysis Exercise

(Answers may vary.)

Score	5	4	3	2	1
Development			V		
Organization				V	
Unity				V	
Language Use			V		

Notes

This response addresses the topic somewhat well but is plagued by a few serious shortcomings. On the positive side, it is fairly well developed with each body paragraph including supporting examples that are moderately developed. In addition, most of the key sentences are fairly clear. What keeps this response from scoring higher is a lack of organization and unity. Each body paragraph fails to present clear arguments. For example, the first body paragraph does not express its main idea—getting

respect by being less polite—until the closing sentences. On top of this, there is a lack of clear transitions between the supporting ideas in each body paragraph. On the whole, this level-3 response could have scored higher if it had better focus.

Final Score: ___3___

Part B
Building Knowledge & Skills for the Writing Test

Education: Football Stadiums

◈ Note-Taking   p.35

1 Main Idea of the Passage: *Schools are justified in spending large amounts of money on their sports teams.*

2 First Supporting Argument: *Modern sports facilities are needed in order to attract a greater number of fans to football games.*

3 Second Supporting Argument: *Schools can increase their revenues by investing in their football teams.*

4 Third Supporting Argument: *A good football team can give troubled youths a reason to stay in school.*

Critical Thinking

1 Schools should spend money in ways that benefit all students.

2 The profits could be used to purchase additional equipment for the school's sports teams or to buy new textbooks and other learning materials. The money could also be used to give teachers salary increases.

◈ Listening   p.36

Script 02-01

Professor: So we've all seen the headlines: "Schools spending millions on football." If you're like me, you see these and wonder to yourself how schools can spend so much on football when they're losing funding for everything else. The truth of the matter is that they can't.

Some people argue that a lot of money needs to be spent on football programs to produce quality teams. That may be true, but does this really affect how enjoyable the games are to watch? By looking at the attendance numbers, you wouldn't think so. In most cases, attendance has remained steady for decades, and in some places, attendance has actually decreased thanks in part to higher ticket prices brought on by the need of these schools to pay for their elaborate stadiums.

And you can guess how teachers feel about all this spending. A recent news article highlighted the, um, twenty million dollars two Texas schools just spent on new football stadiums. At the same time, teachers are getting reductions in their health benefits and losing funding to purchase textbooks for their classes. If a school can't provide teachers with decent benefits, why is it spending millions on football stadiums? It seems as though many school districts are willing to lose talented educators in exchange for jumbotron screens for their stadiums.

You also have to keep in mind the mission of public schools, which is to give all students, regardless of their race, color, creed, social status, or any other factor, an equal education. By pouring millions into football, which, uh, only directly benefits players and coaches, schools are failing to fulfill their main duty. Rather than waste money on a program that has little-to-no academic benefit, these schools must work on maintaining high academic standards so that all students can benefit.

◈ Note-Taking   p.37

1 Main Idea of the Lecture: *Schools cannot afford to spend large amounts of money on their football programs.*

2 First Supporting Argument: *Spending large amounts of money on football programs does not increase game attendance.*

3 Second Supporting Argument: *Schools spend money on stadiums in spite of losing classroom funding.*

4 Third Supporting Argument: *Schools should spend money on programs that directly benefit all students.*

Critical Thinking

1 He explains that attendance at football games has not improved as a result of investing in new stadiums and that investing in football programs does not benefit the entire school, which goes against the mission of public schools.

2 He fails to mention the potential benefits that result from revenues generated by investing in football programs.

Reading	Listening
Main Idea	**Main Idea**
Schools are justified in spending large amounts of money on their sports teams.	*Schools cannot afford to spend large amounts of money on their football programs.*
First Supporting Argument	**First Supporting Argument**
Modern sports facilities are needed in order to attract a greater number of fans to football games.	*Spending large amounts of money on football programs does not increase game attendance.*
Supporting Detail	**Supporting Detail**
new stadium increased football game attendance	*higher prices; attendance decreases*
Second Supporting Argument	**Second Supporting Argument**
Schools can increase their revenues by investing in their football teams.	*Schools spend money on stadiums in spite of losing classroom funding.*
Supporting Detail	**Supporting Detail**
football games; $50,000 income	*waste money on stadiums; lose good teachers*
Third Supporting Argument	**Third Supporting Argument**
A good football team can give troubled youths a reason to stay in school.	*Schools should spend money on programs that directly benefit all students.*
Supporting Detail	**Supporting Detail**
troubled youths stay in school	*spend money for good teachers; benefit all students*

Strong Response   p.40

Critical Analysis

1 The professor's main purpose is to explain why school districts cannot afford to build elaborate football stadiums, and he does so by using three main supporting ideas. / He begins by mentioning the correlation between expensive football stadiums and spectator attendance. / The professor's next point is about funding. / The professor concludes his lecture by bringing up the purpose of public schools, which is to provide an equal education for all.

2 The professor says that most football programs have not seen an increase in attendance for many years

and that some have actually seen a decrease in attendance due to higher ticket prices. / He illustrates this by referencing two schools that each spent twenty million dollars on football stadiums at a time when teachers are losing their benefits and textbook funding. / [T]he lecture states that spending so much money just on football does not give all students the benefits they deserve.

3 He begins by mentioning… The professor's next point is… The professor concludes his lecture by…

Weak Response   p.41

Evaluation

Score	5	4	3	2	1
Development		V			
Organization		V			
Unity		V			
Language Use			V		

Notes

This response is at level 4. It addresses all of the main points of both the lecture and the reading in a fairly organized way. There are a few key problems, though, that keep this from being a level-5 response. The first problem is the lack of clarity. The writer brings up the professor's points, but the unclear language makes it difficult to understand what exactly they are. The next problem is the lack of unity. The response contrasts the reading and the lecture, but it fails to elaborate on the differences between them. The final problems are the minor spelling ("arguement," "professer," etc.) and grammatical errors, which do not interfere with the meaning but can distract the reader.

Final Score: 4

Critical Analysis

Ⓒ

Answer Ⓒ best supports one of the arguments from the lecture. Answers Ⓐ and Ⓑ both contradict the points made in the lecture.

Chapter **01** | Independent Writing

Job Satisfaction vs. High Salary

◈ **Generating Ideas**   p.42

▷ **Agree**

Reason 1: *Earning enough money to live comfortably is*

sufficient.

Reason 2: *Because you spend so much of your time at work, being happy at work makes you healthier in general.*

Reason 3: *People who enjoy their jobs usually work more efficiently.*

▷ **Disagree**

Reason 1: *Earning a high salary prevents any money-related problems from happening.*

Reason 2: *It is easier to live a comfortable, enjoyable life on a higher salary.*

Reason 3: *People who earn high salaries can save enough money to do what they truly enjoy.*

◈ Planning
p.43

Thesis Statement (Agree / Disagree)
While money is certainly important, it is not nearly as important as being satisfied with your work.

First Supporting Idea
As long as you can live comfortably, money should not be an issue.

Supporting Example
compare my middle-income family with my wealthy neighbors

Second Supporting Idea
Job satisfaction is also an important part of a healthy life.

Supporting Example
explain experience working at a high-paying but terrible job

Third Supporting Idea
Finally, liking what you do is essential to working well.

Supporting Example
compare the efficiency of computer programmers who enjoy their work versus programmers who only care about the money

Conclusion
Being happy with your job is more important than earning a large paycheck.

Strong Response
p.45

Critical Analysis

1 While money is certainly important, it is not nearly as important as being satisfied with your work. / As long as you can live comfortably, money should not be

an issue. / Job satisfaction is also an important part of a healthy life. / Liking what you do is essential to working well. / However, being happy with your life is more important than having any amount of money, and it is for this reason that being happy with your job is more important than earning a large paycheck.

2 Although we never vacationed in Europe or owned a luxury sedan, we were happy as a family. / In contrast, our neighbors were quite wealthy. / In spite of their material wealth, their family was not happy. / Although I earn less than half as much money as I used to, I look forward to going to work each morning and now have enough energy to enjoy myself outside of work. / The study showed that those who enjoyed programming were nearly one hundred times more efficient coders that those who became programmers simply to earn a large paycheck.

3 middle-class family compared to wealthy family; the health consequences of working at a deplorable job; efficiency of computer programmers

Weak Response
p.47

Evaluation

Score	5	4	3	2	1
Development				V	
Organization			V		
Unity			V		
Language Use			V		

Notes

This response merits a 3. The main problem is a lack of development. The writer has solid main ideas but fails to support them with enough details and explanations. Another issue is weak unity. The writer fails to integrate the examples given in the second body paragraph (the happiness of Warren Buffet and Bill Gates) while the essay lacks strong transitions between its ideas. Finally, the grammatical errors prevent this essay from scoring higher.

Final Score: ___3___

Critical Analysis

Ⓐ

Answer Ⓐ best supports the central idea of the response and could easily be used as the topic sentence for the third body paragraph. Answer Ⓑ directly contradicts the thesis while Answer Ⓒ does not adequately support it.

Political Science: The Monroe Doctrine

◈ Note-Taking   p.51

1 Main Idea of the Passage: *The Monroe Doctrine has allowed nations throughout the Americas to maintain their independence.*

2 First Supporting Argument: *The doctrine allowed the United States to expand its sphere of influence throughout the Americas.*

3 Second Supporting Argument: *The United States relied on the doctrine to prevent further colonization of the Americas by European powers.*

4 Third Supporting Argument: *The Monroe Doctrine helped promote political stability in Latin America.*

Critical Thinking

1 By keeping European powers out of the Americas, the U.S. was able to expand its own sphere of influence without competition from other powerful nations.

2 No, I do not think the doctrine helped other nations become independent because the U.S. seemed to use the doctrine to justify sending its military to gain control of other nations in the Americas.

◈ Listening   p.52

Script 02-02

Professor: Um, as you know, the Monroe Doctrine was created by the U.S. to defend smaller nations throughout the Americas from European colonization. But if this was the case, then why did it seem primarily to protect the interests of the U.S.?

Well, first of all . . . the United States was not a powerful country at the time, so it created the doctrine as a way to become a major player on the global stage. However, it's not so readily apparent that the doctrine helped the U.S. gain any, um, international authority. On the contrary, the doctrine was almost a cry for the attention of then-superpower Great Britain. In fact, the only reason the doctrine was able to be enforced at all was that Great Britain tacitly supported it.

But that's not to imply that the doctrine did not fulfill its intended purpose. The U.S. was a rapidly growing nation yearning for more clout, and under the guise of checking colonization, it relied on the doctrine to usurp vast expanses of territory from Spain. By keeping the European powers at bay, the U.S. used the doctrine to fulfill its Manifest Destiny . . . the idea that U.S. territory should extend from the east coast to the west coast.

Clearly, there was a double standard at work.

So what ultimately became of the doctrine? Over the next several decades, the U.S. relied on it to establish, uh, hegemony throughout the Americas. Perhaps the most notable instance of this occurred in 1895, where the U.S. threatened to take strong action against Great Britain if it failed to resolve its dispute with Venezuela. Although the British prime minister initially objected to the demands of the U.S., he did not, um, push the issue further when the U.S. stood its ground. As a result, historians view this as the final concession by European powers of the U.S.'s dominance over the Americas.

◈ Note-Taking   p.53

1 Main Idea of the Lecture: *The Monroe Doctrine was created for the benefit of the United States.*

2 First Supporting Argument: *The Monroe Doctrine did not help the U.S. gain international authority.*

3 Second Supporting Argument: *The doctrine was used to justify Manifest Destiny.*

4 Third Supporting Argument: *The U.S. relied on the doctrine to establish hegemony throughout the Americas.*

Critical Thinking

1 The lecturer refutes all of the arguments from the reading. It says that the doctrine did not allow the U.S. to gain any international authority, that the U.S. was not primarily interested in stopping colonization, and that the U.S. used the doctrine to gain some measure of control over Latin American nations.

2 She does a thorough job of refuting the points made in the reading.

◈ Tandem Note-Taking

p.54

Reading	Listening
Main Idea *The Monroe Doctrine has allowed nations throughout the Americas to maintain their independence.*	**Main Idea** *The Monroe Doctrine was created for the benefit of the United States.*
First Supporting Argument *The doctrine allowed the United States to expand its sphere of influence throughout the Americas.*	**First Supporting Argument** *The Monroe Doctrine did not help the U.S. gain international authority.*
Supporting Detail *could not colonize without retribution from U.S.*	**Supporting Detail** *gained the support of Great Britain*
Second Supporting Argument *The United States relied on the doctrine to prevent further colonization of the Americas by European powers.*	**Second Supporting Argument** *The doctrine was used to justify Manifest Destiny.*
Supporting Detail *European powers no colonization*	**Supporting Detail** *gained lots of land from Spain*
Third Supporting Argument *The Monroe Doctrine helped promote political stability in Latin America.*	**Third Supporting Argument** *The U.S. relied on the doctrine to establish hegemony throughout the Americas.*
Supporting Detail *1870s; prevented European powers from interfering*	**Supporting Detail** *Great Britain/Venezuela dispute*

Strong Response

p.56

Critical Analysis

1 Her arguments largely refute the points made in the reading passage. / The lecturer begins by agreeing with the reading's assertion that the U.S. was not a powerful nation when the doctrine was introduced. / The professor's next point is about the relationship between the doctrine and colonization. / Finally, the instructor argues that the doctrine was used to establish U.S. hegemony throughout the Americas.

2 She says there is little evidence that the doctrine helped the U.S. gain any international authority and that it was created primarily to get the attention of

Great Britain, which was the world's most powerful country at the time. / As the lecturer noted, the doctrine kept European powers out of the Americas, thereby allowing the U.S. to seize vast amounts of land from France and Spain and to carry out its goal of Manifest Destiny. / She illustrates this by mentioning how the U.S. relied on the doctrine to intervene on the conflict between Venezuela and Great Britain.

3 The lecturer begins by… The lecturer's next point is… Finally, the instructor argues that…

Weak Response

p.57

Evaluation

Score	5	4	3	2	1
Development			V		
Organization		V			
Unity			V		
Language Use			V		

Notes
This is a level-3 response. It features fairly strong organization, with each body paragraph focusing on the main ideas from the reading passage and lecture in a relatively clear manner. What holds this response back are the lack of development and the fact that it fails to explain which arguments come from the reading passage and which come from the lecture. In addition, the grammatical mistakes, while minor when taken individually, are frequent enough to distract the reader.

Final Score: ___3___

Critical Analysis

Answer Ⓒ is the best choice because it provides a specific example from the lecture while explaining where it came from. Answer Ⓐ is incorrect because it explains one of the points from the reading passage, but this response would benefit from having more detail about the lecture. Answer Ⓑ is also incorrect because it is a general statement that does not provide the level of detail needed to improve this response.

Broad Knowledge vs. Specialized Knowledge

◉ Generating Ideas
p.58

▷ **Broad Knowledge**

Reason 1: *Having broad knowledge can make it easier to solve problems because you develop a broad understanding of many fields.*

Reason 2: *By receiving a broad education, you learn about a wide variety of subjects. In this way, you are able to discover which subjects interest you the most.*

Reason 3: *With a broad knowledge base, you can solve problems across many fields.*

▷ **Specialized Knowledge**

Reason 1: *Specialized knowledge allows you to develop a high level of mastery in one area.*

Reason 2: *Many high-paying jobs require specialized knowledge, making it financially beneficial.*

Reason 3: *Having specialized knowledge gives you a greater sense of purpose in life.*

◉ Planning
p.59

Thesis Statement (Broad Knowledge / Specialized Knowledge)

A specialized education is much more beneficial.

First Supporting Idea

Specializing in one area allows you to master a subject.

Supporting Example

Many fields require the mastery of a deep set of skills.

Second Supporting Idea

Individuals with specialized skills are able to land lucrative jobs more easily.

Supporting Example

Many high-paying jobs require specialized knowledge.

Third Supporting Idea

Professionals with specialized knowledge tend to have a greater sense of purpose in life.

Supporting Example

Explain the situations of two friends who recently graduated from college.

Conclusion

For most people, obtaining a specialized education is much more beneficial as it can lead to a high-paying career and give a greater sense of purpose in life.

Strong Response
p.61

Critical Analysis

1 A specialized education is much more beneficial. / Specializing in one area allows you to master a subject. / Individuals with specialized skills are able to land lucrative jobs more easily. / Professionals with specialized knowledge tend to have a greater sense of purpose in life.

2 Fields such as pharmacology and accounting require the mastery of a deep set of skills. Anything less than complete understanding in these fields is unacceptable. / Many of today's highest-paying jobs, such as engineer and computer programmer, require specialized knowledge. / The journalism friend has not been able to find a steady job that he enjoys while the engineering friend recently started a high-paying career as a nuclear engineer. / The journalism friend always complains about how meaningless his life is.

3 an engineer designing a bridge; a computer programmer writing code; the journalism student not having purpose in life; the engineering student enjoying life

---

Weak Response
p.63

Evaluation

Score	5	4	3	2	1
Development			V		
Organization		V			
Unity		V			
Language Use		V			

Notes
In spite of some shortcomings, this is a strong response overall. The thesis statement is clear and well written as are most of the topic sentences. The paragraphs are nicely organized, and the transitions between them are smooth. Although there are a few grammatical and spelling mistakes (e.g. "peoples" instead of people's, "inerresting" instead of interesting), they do not interfere with the meaning. The only major weakness is a slight lack of development caused by some unclear examples. Overall, though, the writer's intent is clear, which is why this response merits a 4.

Final Score: __4__

Critical Analysis

Ⓐ

Answer Ⓐ would best strengthen the response. Answer Ⓑ contradicts the central idea of the response while

Answer Ⓒ is a specific fact that cannot be developed easily.

Engineering: The Tacoma Narrows Bridge

◈ Note-Taking
p.67

1 Main Idea of the Passage: *The Tacoma Narrows Bridge collapsed due to aerodynamic instability.*

2 First Supporting Argument: *The extremely narrow width of the main span of the bridge in relation to its length allowed the bridge to twist, thus causing it to collapse.*

3 Second Supporting Argument: *A lack of support cables contributed to the twisting motion, therefore contributing to the collapse of the bridge.*

4 Third Supporting Argument: *The bridge would not have collapsed had it been built out of stronger materials.*

Critical Thinking

1 These solid plates probably contributed to the collapse because they allowed the wind to move the roadbed more easily.

2 It is possible to infer from the last sentence that the designers felt concrete was too heavy a building material.

◈ Listening
p.68

Script 02-03

Professor: All right, class, today I want to discuss the importance of aerodynamics in bridge design. Now, you are aware of the famous Tacoma Narrows Bridge collapse, but you might not be aware of the role the bridge's design played in the collapse.

Let me start off by addressing the issue of the bridge's width. It's true that the main span of the bridge was very narrow, but this wasn't the reason why it collapsed. Galloping Gertie was the first bridge to employ plate girders to support the roadbed. These poorly designed plates were not at all aerodynamic and actually presented an obstacle for the wind. So even if the engineers had quadrupled the width of the span, that would have done little to prevent the self-excited vibrations that ultimately led to the bridge's failure.

Another factor cited as a major cause of the collapse was the lack of support cables. While it's true that the slippage of one of the support cables contributed to the failure of the structure, there is little evidence to suggest that having an, uh, insufficient amount of support cables was a principal cause. Actually, given the amount of force created by the twisting road surface, even having twice as many cables would not have prevented the swaying from occurring.

The last point I would like to mention is the bridge's building material. Undoubtedly, the bridge would still be standing today had it been built with steel-reinforced concrete. However, it is shortsighted to suggest that the bridge fell simply because it was built out of steel. Again, design was the determining factor. Had a truss design been used for the roadbed, the bridge would have remained intact because it would have easily allowed air to pass through . . . and the bridge would have been much more aerodynamic as a result.

◈ Note-Taking
p.69

1 Main Idea of the Lecture: *A flawed design caused the Tacoma Narrows Bridge to collapse.*

2 First Supporting Argument: *The use of plate girders that were not aerodynamic contributed to the structural failure of the bridge.*

3 Second Supporting Argument: *There is little evidence to suggest that a lack of support cables contributed to the collapse of the bridge.*

4 Third Supporting Argument: *The use of an aerodynamic truss design would have prevented the bridge's collapse.*

Critical Thinking

1 The lecture explains that the use of solid steel plates to support the roadbed contributed to the collapse more than the narrowness of the main span. It also mentions that increasing the number of cables would not likely have prevented the collapse and that the design of the roadbed contributed more to causing the collapse than the use of steel did.

2 He mentions the plate girders, which presented an obstacle for the wind. He also talks about the extreme force of the twisting motion. Finally, he mentions the truss design and how it would have made the bridge stronger.

Reading	Listening
Main Idea	**Main Idea**
The Tacoma Narrows Bridge collapsed due to aerodynamic instability.	*A flawed design caused the Tacoma Narrows Bridge to collapse.*
First Supporting Argument	**First Supporting Argument**
The extremely narrow width of the main span of the bridge in relation to its length allowed the bridge to twist, thus causing it to collapse.	*The use of plate girders that were not aerodynamic contributed to the structural failure of the bridge.*
Supporting Detail	**Supporting Detail**
self-perpetuating twisting motion; could not rest	*quadrupling width of span would not have helped*
Second Supporting Argument	**Second Supporting Argument**
A lack of support cables contributed to the twisting motion, therefore contributing to the collapse of the bridge.	*There is little evidence to suggest that a lack of support cables contributed to the collapse of the bridge.*
Supporting Detail	**Supporting Detail**
support cables down twenty-five percent	*doubling number of support cables would not have helped*
Third Supporting Argument	**Third Supporting Argument**
The bridge would not have collapsed had it been built out of stronger materials.	*The use of an aerodynamic truss design would have prevented the bridge's collapse.*
Supporting Detail	**Supporting Detail**
concrete bridges stronger	*truss design; wind pass easily*

Strong Response p.72

Critical Analysis

1 The lecture posits that the bridge collapsed due to a flawed design, which runs contrary to the points made in the reading passage. / [T]he professor questions the reading's assessment that having a narrow main span contributed to the collapse of the Tacoma Narrows Bridge. / The professor then moves on to the issue of the lack of support cables. / The professor concludes his lecture by discussing the bridge's building materials.

2 He says that the width of the bridge could not affect the bridge's structural integrity in any way. / He

does admit that a lack of support cables may have contributed to the collapse, but he believes that the twisting was so severe that even doubling the number of support cables would not have prevented the collapse. / Had the bridge employed the more aerodynamic truss design, it would have remained standing to this day.

3 To begin with… The professor then moves on to… The professor concludes his lecture by…

Weak Response p.73

Evaluation

Score	5	4	3	2	1
Development		V			
Organization		V			
Unity		V			
Language Use			V		

Notes

This response does a good job of interweaving points from the reading and the lecture. The strong organization and the good use of transitions generally make the essay easy to understand. There are a few factors preventing this essay from scoring a 5 though. While the response is generally clear, the key sentence in the second body paragraph ("However, the professor says that not enough cables was not problem, because the force of the road was too much for the cables to handle.") is difficult to follow. The response also contains several spelling errors ("aeordynamic," "callapse"), misused words ("wideness"), shifts in verb tense, and other assorted errors that distract the reader.

Final Score: ___4___

Critical Analysis

Ⓐ

Answer Ⓐ is the best choice because it provides more detail from the lecture, which would help address the task of summarizing the lecture. Answers Ⓑ and Ⓒ are not correct because they are based on the arguments presented in the reading passage.

Making Decisions

◈ Generating Ideas p.74

▷ **Agree**

Reason 1: *Consulting with others can allow you to*

consider your situation from a different perspective.

Reason 2: *When you get advice from others, you are able to consider many different possible solutions.*

Reason 3: *Getting suggestions from others can allow you to make your decision confidently.*

▷ **Disagree**

Reason 1: *Getting advice from others can slow down the decision-making process.*

Reason 2: *Only you know what is best for yourself.*

Reason 3: *People might consider you indecisive and weak willed if you cannot make decisions alone.*

◈ Planning
p.75

Thesis Statement (Agree / Disagree)
I believe it is essential to consult with others when making important decisions.

First Supporting Idea
One of the strongest arguments in favor of consulting with others is the issue of impact.

Supporting Example
A major decision such as getting married can affect the lives of many others.

Second Supporting Idea
There is also the issue of gaining new perspectives.

Supporting Example
Even U.S. presidents get advice from others when making decisions.

Third Supporting Idea
Finally, there is the issue of confidence.

Supporting Example
Getting approval from others makes the decision-making process easier.

Conclusion
It is imperative to get advice from others when making important decisions.

Strong Response
p.77

Critical Analysis

1 I believe it is essential to consult with others when making important decisions. / One of the strongest arguments in favor of consulting with others is the issue of impact. / Impact is not the sole justification for consulting others, however; there is also the issue of gaining new perspectives. / Finally, there is the

issue of confidence.

2 I recently got married. / This decision impacted not only my life but also the lives of my husband and our families. / In this situation, I was not able to make my decision alone. / Rather, I had to consult with the people who would be affected by the outcome of my decision to marry before I could make my decision. / Even high-ranking leaders, such as the president of the United States, seek the opinions of others before making decisions. / For instance, I once considered changing my career, but I was not confident that it was a wise decision to do so.

3 the impact of marriage on the couple and their families; leaders ask others from advice; not being able to execute a plan due to a lack of self-confidence

Weak Response
p.79

Evaluation

Score	5	4	3	2	1
Development				V	
Organization			V		
Unity				V	
Language Use				V	

Notes

This response has a lot of shortcomings that hold it back. Although it features decent organization bolstered by the use of transitional phrases between ideas, it is weakened by a lack of development and poor explanations. The example for the third supporting idea is especially difficult to understand. Furthermore, the overall level of grammar and vocabulary is quite low, and the numerous typing errors make the response more difficult to read. For these reasons, this response earns a 2.

Final Score: ___2___

Critical Analysis

Answer Ⓑ is the best choice because body paragraph 2 argues that asking for the advice of others can slow down the decision-making process and prevent people from getting what they want.

Environmental Science: Land Reclamation

◊ Note-Taking   p.83

1   Main Idea of the Passage: *Land reclamation provides a number of benefits.*

2   First Supporting Argument: *The primary advantage is that it increases the amount of usable land in an area.*

3   Second Supporting Argument: *Reclaimed land almost always borders the ocean or the sea.*

4   Third Supporting Argument: *Land reclamation helps provide individuals with areas where they can have residences.*

Critical Thinking

1   I think land reclamation is fine because it gives people more places to live, and it also helps get rid of places like swamps.

2   It fails to explain what happens to the fish and other creatures that used to live in the areas where the islands are created.

◊ Listening   p.84

Script 02-04

Professor: Did you see that the government is planning to drain some of the local swamps by the seashore in an effort to reclaim the land? I have to tell you . . . That's a horrible idea. Land reclamation has several negative issues.

First of all, much of the land that is reclaimed around the world is wetlands. These include marshes, bogs, swamps, and mangrove forests. Those areas serve a very important purpose. They help prevent flooding, especially during tropical storms. Wetlands can take in huge amounts of water, and mangrove forests are great at stopping storm surges. If that land is reclaimed, we're likely going to get some bad flooding during future storms.

Another problem with land reclamation is that nowadays, it's often done in order to create artificial islands. Well, uh, some of the places where those islands are made used to be coral reefs. Coral reefs are incredibly valuable ecosystems. Huge numbers of marine species live in them. They also use coral reefs as breeding grounds. Land reclamation is directly harming our ocean ecosystems in many places.

Finally, I know that the city plans to build some apartment complexes on the reclaimed land. But what about the animals that live there now? They're going to

be displaced when the wetlands are destroyed. Some endangered birds live there, and lots of migratory birds use those wetlands to find food. We're going to be causing a tremendous amount of harm to local wildlife if that land is reclaimed. It's entirely possible that a couple of species will go extinct if those wetlands are destroyed.

◊ Note-Taking   p.85

1   Main Idea of the Lecture: *Land reclamation has several negative issues.*

2   First Supporting Argument: *Wetlands help prevent flooding and are great at stopping storm surges.*

3   Second Supporting Argument: *Many of the places where there are artificial islands used to be coral reefs.*

4   Third Supporting Argument: *Animals living on reclaimed land are displaced.*

Critical Thinking

1   The lecturer states that reclaimed land is often wetlands and that wetlands are important because they can prevent flooding and stop storm surges. She also mentions that artificial islands are often in areas where coral reefs used to be. Coral reefs are important marine ecosystems. Finally, she adds that animals get displaced when land is reclaimed by people.

2   The lecturer mentions that mangrove forests are great at stopping storm surges. She points out that coral reefs have many marine species living in them and are used as breeding grounds. She states that endangered birds may live in wetlands that are reclaimed and that some species might go extinct due to land reclamation.

◊ Tandem Note-Taking

Reading	Listening
Main Idea	**Main Idea**
Land reclamation provides a number of benefits.	*Land reclamation has several negative issues.*
First Supporting Argument	**First Supporting Argument**
Land reclamation increases the amount of usable land in an area.	*Wetlands help prevent flooding and are great at stopping storm surges.*
Supporting Detail	**Supporting Detail**
used as farmland and residential areas	*effective during tropical storms; mangrove forests*
Second Supporting Argument	**Second Supporting Argument**
Reclaimed land almost always borders the ocean or the sea.	*Many of the places where there are artificial islands used to be coral reefs.*
Supporting Detail	**Supporting Detail**
is very valuable; makes land reclamation profitable	*huge numbers of marine species; used as breeding grounds*
Third Supporting Argument	**Third Supporting Argument**
Land reclamation helps provide individuals with areas where they can have residences.	*Animals living on reclaimed land are displaced.*
Supporting Detail	**Supporting Detail**
global population increasing; places like Singapore need land so that people are not so cramped	*migratory birds use wetlands to find food; some species may go extinct*

◊ Strong Response

p.88

Critical Analysis

1 In her lecture, the professor casts doubt on the points made in the reading passage. / To begin, the professor notes that much reclaimed land used to be wetlands. / Next, the professor discusses how artificial islands are recovered from reclaimed land. / Last, the professor tells the class about the danger to local wildlife when land is reclaimed.

2 She claims these areas, which include swamps and mangrove forests, are effective at preventing flooding as well as stopping storm surges. / She believes flooding will be a problem in the future if some land is reclaimed. / While the reading passage states that these islands are valuable land since they border the sea, the professor does not think creating artificial

islands is a good idea. / She points out that many used to be coral reefs, which are important to marine ecosystems. / She says some endangered birds live in an area which is going to be reclaimed. / She argues that some species there may go extinct, too.

3 In her lecture, the professor… In this way, she… Next, the professor… Last, the professor…

Weak Response

p.89

Evaluation

Score	5	4	3	2	1
Development				V	
Organization				V	
Unity				V	
Language Use			V		

Notes

This is a poor response that does not follow the instructions. It has several factual mistakes, including claiming that the professor supports reclaiming land to create artificial islands. In addition, in the third paragraph, the test taker includes personal thoughts in the essay. ("I like the reading. I think the reading has the best ideas.") Personal thoughts should never be included in an essay. Finally, the sentences are very simple in form and contain many mistakes. This is a level-2 response.

Final Score: 2

Critical Analysis

Answer is the best choice because it explains the professor's argument regarding artificial islands. Answers Ⓑ and Ⓒ both contain arguments that are not made in the lecture and are therefore incorrect.

Chapter 04 | Independent Writing

Leisure Time

◊ Generating Ideas

p.90

▷ **Agree**

Reason 1: *Technology makes life more efficient, so the amount of leisure time that people have has increased.*

Reason 2: *Work schedules have become shorter and more flexible, and as a result, people now have more leisure time.*

Reason 3: *Today, relaxation and leisure time have an*

increasing amount of importance with many people.

▷ **Disagree**

Reason 1: *Some technology has made it more difficult for people to relax and to have leisure time.*

Reason 2: *As people become more competitive, they must spend more time improving themselves and their credentials.*

Reason 3: *Because people's spending habits have increased, they have to spend more time working in order to maintain their lifestyle.*

◈ Planning

p.91

Thesis Statement (Agree / Disagree)
People will have more leisure time in the future than they do today.

First Supporting Idea
One of the key developments leading to this increase in leisure time has been changes to work culture.

Supporting Example
The number of hours people work has decreased over time.

Second Supporting Idea
The main factor that has brought about such changes in the workplace is technology.

Supporting Example
Cell phones and the Internet have made work more efficient.

Conclusion
But thanks to changes in the workplace brought on by changes to work culture and developments in technology, people can now afford to spend most of their time relaxing.

Strong Response
p.93

Critical Analysis

1 As a result, people will have more leisure time in the future than they do today. / One of the key developments leading to this increase in leisure time has been changes to work culture. / The main factor that has brought about such changes in the workplace is technology. / But thanks to changes in the workplace brought on by changes to work culture and developments in technology, people can now afford to spend most of their time relaxing.

2 In the past, many people worked twelve or more hours per day, seven days per week, doing difficult work such as coal mining or farming. / Today, more and more people have task-based positions that give them greater flexibility in when, where, and how much they work. In the future, these types of jobs will become more common, thus leading to increased leisure time. / Developments in technology, such as cell phones, the Internet, and even robotic tractors, have made older jobs more efficient while creating new jobs that are less tedious and time consuming. / No longer do people have to spend hours driving to their destination or riding on a slow-moving train. / Technology such as the jetliner and the bullet train has made traveling more efficient and allow people to spend their free time as they should: relaxing.

3 changes to the number of hours people work; technology that has made life more efficient

Weak Response
p.95

Evaluation

Score	5	4	3	2	1
Development	V				
Organization	V				
Unity		V			
Language Use		V			

Notes

This is a strong response. It has a clear topic sentence, good development of its supporting ideas, a strong organization, and a high level of unity. What keeps this response from earning a 5, however, are the errors in language use, such as "lifes" instead of "lives" and "more wealthy" instead of "wealthy." Although none of these grammatical errors hinders the reader individually, their frequency does distract the reader and lessens the overall impact of the response.

Final Score: __4__

Critical Analysis

Ⓑ

Answer Ⓑ best expresses the idea of the highlighted sentence. Both Answers Ⓐ and Ⓒ misrepresent the idea of the highlighted sentence.

Literature: People Read Less Literature Today

◊ Note-Taking
p.99

1 Main Idea of the Passage: *The movement away from reading literature has negatively affected society.*

2 First Supporting Argument: *Literature develops the imagination.*

3 Second Supporting Argument: *Literature sustains and develops culture.*

4 Third Supporting Argument: *Most people are too lazy to read literature.*

Critical Thinking

1 Television, movies, and music can all reflect and develop culture.

2 No, I do not think so because films and television can inspire wonder with their unique, visually appealing worlds. Listening to music can also cause people to create images in their minds.

◊ Listening
p.100

Script 02-05

Professor: You know, a lot of groups out there are lamenting the decline in literary reading among adults of all age groups. They say that this will result in nothing short of cultural genocide. Sounds pretty horrific, right? Well, in reality, the decline in literary reading is not as tragic as it's made out to be.

Yes, it's true that people aren't reading as much literature as they used to. But that's not to say that people aren't reading at all anymore. On the contrary, the number of people who read has actually increased. And these people aren't simply reading tabloids and comic books; many of today's best-selling works are multifaceted scientific, political, and historical texts. While these sorts of writings may not develop the imagination as much as, say, a Charles Dickens novel, they are, um, nevertheless intellectually stimulating and engaging.

In addition, there are many other forms of nonliterary activity, such as listening to music and watching television. Not only do these other activities offer genuine entertainment, but they also provide people with a multitude of creative outlets that simply didn't exist a century ago. Really, the decrease in literary reading is due to cultural changes brought about by advances in technology. Television, movies, music, and even video games all develop culture much in the same way that novels and others forms of literature do.

And don't blame the readers for reading less literature. Many of today's literary works are too abstruse to be enjoyed. What I mean is, um, most pieces of literature are simply overly complex and cannot be understood easily. I mean, think about it. When you look for entertainment, you want to find a relaxing way to escape the monotony of everyday life. But because a lot of literature requires so much effort on the part of the reader, many people find they simply cannot enjoy it.

◊ Note-Taking
p.101

1 Main Idea of the Lecture: *The decline in literary reading is not that serious a problem.*

2 First Supporting Argument: *More people read today than before.*

3 Second Supporting Argument: *There are other forms of nonliterary activity.*

4 Third Supporting Argument: *Many of today's literary works are too complex.*

Critical Thinking

1 The lecturer largely refutes the points in the reading in saying that other forms of writing develop the imagination and critical thinking skills. Next, she mentions that other forms of media develop culture. Finally, she says that most literature is too difficult to enjoy as relaxing entertainment.

2 She does not completely refute the reading's argument that people do not read literature because they are lazy.

◈ Tandem Note-Taking

p.102

Reading	Listening
Main Idea *The movement away from reading literature has negatively affected society.*	**Main Idea** *The decline in literary reading is not that serious a problem.*
First Supporting Argument *Literature sustains and develops culture.*	**First Supporting Argument** *More people read today than before.*
Supporting Detail *historical record of culture*	**Supporting Detail** *difficult science, political and history texts*
Second Supporting Argument *Literature develops the imagination.*	**Second Supporting Argument** *There are other forms of nonliterary activity.*
Supporting Detail *readers visualize worlds in novels*	**Supporting Detail** *television, movies, music, and video games develop culture*
Third Supporting Argument *Most people are too lazy to read literature.*	**Third Supporting Argument** *Many of today's literary works are too complex.*
Supporting Detail *modern entertainment not engaging*	**Supporting Detail** *relax during free time*

Strong Response
p.104

Critical Analysis

1 She presents information that suggests the decline is not harmful and thus contradicts the reading passage's claim that the shift away from reading literature has negatively affected society. / First of all, the lecturer says that while people are not reading as much as they used to, the total number of people who read has risen. / Another main point is that many other forms of nonliterary activities, such as music and television, exist. / Finally, the professor explains that the decrease in literary reading may be caused by the books themselves.

2 The professor goes on to explain that today's most popular books are deep, multifaceted texts. / She further asserts that these texts are intellectually stimulating and engaging. / The professor argues that these forms of media offer not only entertainment but also additional creative outlets. / She further contends that the decrease in reading is the result of cultural changes and that these new forms of media develop culture in the same way novels do. /

She explains that a majority of literary works are too difficult to be enjoyed and that a lot of people want a relaxing way to spend their free time.

3 First of all… The professor goes on to explain… She further asserts… Another main point is… She further contends… Finally…

Weak Response
p.105

Evaluation

Score	5	4	3	2	1
Development			V		
Organization			V		
Unity				V	
Language Use				V	

Notes

This response has a few key shortcomings that keep it from scoring higher. On the positive side, it mentions all of the points from the listening passage although it misrepresents a few of the ideas. However, the fundamental flaw with this response is its failure to make connections between the listening and reading. The weak grammar, the numerous spelling mistakes, and the confusing sentences further detract from the response. Overall, this response earns a 3.

Final Score: __3__

Critical Analysis

Ⓑ

Answer Ⓑ is the best choice because it most accurately summarizes the argument presented in the reading passage. Answer Ⓐ is not mentioned in either the reading passage or the lecture while Answer Ⓒ is not directly stated in the reading passage.

Chapter **05** | Independent Writing

Keeping Up with World Events

◈ Generating Ideas
p.106

▷ **Agree**

Reason 1: *Learning about global news events can teach you about issues that affect people around the globe, which allows you to better understand similar events in your area.*

Reason 2: *Events that occur in other nations, such as viral outbreaks and wars, have the potential to spread around the globe.*

Reason 3: *People should care about the plights of others even if they do not know the other people.*

▷ **Disagree**

Reason 1: *Most people are very busy with their daily obligations to follow world events.*

Reason 2: *To understand events in other places properly, you must have some knowledge of the country and its history.*

Reason 3: *News stories are inherently shocking and tragic, so following world news events can cause unnecessary negative emotions.*

◈ Planning
p.107

Thesis Statement (Agree / Disagree)
People should not follow world events that do not relate to them.

First Supporting Idea
Most people are consumed with the events in their own lives.

Supporting Example
On a typical day, most people have to do several errands.

Second Supporting Idea
Related to this is the issue of unnecessary emotional burdens.

Supporting Example
News stories are emotionally taxing.

Third Supporting Idea
Even if people were to follow news stories that do not affect them, they would not be able to understand the true nature of the events.

Supporting Example
Understanding the significance of events such as economic situations or political elections requires a profound knowledge of a country's history, culture, and language.

Conclusion
But for the reasons given above, it is better to remain unaware of world news events that have no bearing on your life.

Strong Response
p.109

Critical Analysis

1 For the following three reasons, I do not believe so. / For one, most people are consumed with the events

in their own lives. / Related to this is the issue of unnecessary emotional burdens. / Even if people were to follow news stories that do not affect them, they would not be able to understand the true nature of the events. / For the reasons given above, it is better to remain unaware of world news events that have no bearing on your life.

2 On a typical day, most people have to do several errands, such as dropping their kids off at school, finishing a report before a meeting, having lunch with a new business client, or being on time for soccer practice. / News stories are such because they are shocking, tragic, or horrific. / Most people already have enough stress in their lives, and following news stories from around the world would only add to this emotional burden. / Understanding the significance of events such as economic situations or political elections requires a profound knowledge of a country's history, culture, and language. / Outsiders with no connection to the country simply cannot fathom these types of events.

3 daily activities in people's lives; emotionally taxing nature of news stories; difficulty in understanding the significance of story without knowing a nation's culture

Weak Response
p.111

Evaluation

Score	5	4	3	2	1
Development			V		
Organization				V	
Unity				V	
Language Use				V	

Notes

This response is more developed than most level-2 responses, with two of the body paragraphs including examples to illustrate supporting ideas. What keeps this essay from scoring higher is a lack of coherence between paragraphs. The third body paragraph fails to relate to the topic in any meaningful way while the poor grammar in other paragraphs ("If someone gets an disease in the other place, they know suddenly show aobut getting the disease") make it difficult for the reader to understand the ideas the writer is trying to present.

Final Score: __2__

Critical Analysis

Ⓒ

Answer Ⓒ is the best choice because body paragraph 3

mentions empathy and the idea of caring for other people.

Environmental Studies: Green Consumerism

◈ Note-Taking
p.115

1 Main Idea of the Passage: *Green consumerism will prevent environmental destruction.*

2 First Supporting Argument: *Green consumerism is an easy way for people to help protect the environment.*

3 Second Supporting Argument: *Green consumerism benefits consumers because green products are of a higher quality than regular products.*

4 Third Supporting Argument: *Green consumerism leads to other types of environmental activism.*

Critical Thinking

1 They might have drawbacks such as environmentally damaging production and transportation methods and higher prices than regular products.

2 It might cause people to believe that green consumerism is enough to protect the environment. As a result, they might stop doing other things that are more helpful for the environment, such as reducing consumption.

◈ Listening
p.116

Script 02-06

Professor: Um, so let me pose a question: Is green consumerism as beneficial as it's made out to be? Well, it's a complicated issue, but let me start by addressing some common misconceptions.

All right, so there's a prevailing notion that by making a few small changes to your shopping habits, you can help curb environmental destruction and climate change. Unfortunately, this isn't really the case. Let me give you an example. If every person in the world bought only green products for an entire year, the reduction in pollutants would only be equivalent to one power plant shutting down for one day. In other words, the environmental benefits of green consumerism are so minute that they aren't even beneficial.

Another belief is the idea that green products perform in a manner that is superior to regular products. Um . . . some green products, such as hybrid cars, perform better than conventional products. But most green products have something called a hidden cost. That's when a product has a disadvantage that outweighs

its advantages. For instance, take compact florescent light bulbs. Although they have a much greater lifespan than regular light bulbs, they are made by using toxins and other carcinogens that can severely damage the environment if they are not disposed of properly. In short, many supposedly green products may not be helpful to the environment at all.

Last, there is the notion that green consumerism drives people to become more environmentally active. Well, that may be true for some people, but most people, um, develop a false sense of complacency. That is to say, they think shopping green is enough to help save the environment. As a result, these people are less likely to recycle, to reduce consumption, or to use alternative energy sources . . . all things that make sizable contributions to protecting the environment.

◈ Note–Taking
p.117

1 Main Idea of the Lecture: *Green consumerism may not be as beneficial as it is thought to be.*

2 First Supporting Argument: *Making small changes to your shopping and consuming habits is not effective at preventing environmental destruction.*

3 Second Supporting Argument: *Most green products do not offer performances better than those of regular products.*

4 Third Supporting Argument: *Green consumerism does not cause people to become more environmentally active.*

Critical Thinking

1 The professor dispels the notion that small changes to shopping habits can curb environmental destruction. He also refutes the idea that all green products have performances superior to those of regular products and that green consumerism causes people to become more environmentally active.

2 The professor fails to discredit all of the possible environmental benefits of green consumerism.

♦ Tandem Note-Taking

Reading	Listening
Main Idea	**Main Idea**
Green consumerism will prevent environmental destruction.	*Green consumerism may not be as beneficial as it is thought to be.*
First Supporting Argument	**First Supporting Argument**
Green consumerism is an easy way for people to help protect the environment.	*Making small changes to your shopping and consuming habits is not effective at preventing environmental destruction.*
Supporting Detail	**Supporting Detail**
reduce landfill waste by ten percent	*green consumerism is like shutting down one power plant for a day*
Second Supporting Argument	**Second Supporting Argument**
Green consumerism benefits consumers because green products are of a higher quality than regular products.	*Most green products do not offer performances better than those of regular products.*
Supporting Detail	**Supporting Detail**
fluorescent light bulbs last five times longer	*hidden costs; carcinogens in fluorescent light bulbs*
Third Supporting Argument	**Third Supporting Argument**
Green consumerism leads to other types of environmental activism.	*Green consumerism does not cause people to become more environmentally active.*
Supporting Detail	**Supporting Detail**
creates domino effect	*less likely to recycle or to reduce consumption*

Strong Response

p.120

Critical Analysis

1 In the listening, the lecturer makes arguments that contradict the points made in the reading. / The lecturer begins by discrediting the notion that people can curb environmental destruction by making only small changes to their shopping habits. / Next, the lecturer refutes the belief that green products offer superior performances over those of regular products. / The lecturer concludes by explaining that green consumerism does not lead people to become more environmentally active and that most green consumers are less likely to recycle or to use alternative energy sources.

2 He illustrates this by explaining that if every person on the planet bought only green products for a year, it would only reduce pollutants as much as the shutting down of a single power plant for one day. / He explains that most green products have a hidden cost and illustrates this by mentioning the carcinogens contained in florescent light bulbs. / The lecturer concludes by explaining that green consumerism does not lead people to become more environmentally active and that most green consumers are less likely to recycle or to use alternative energy sources.

3 The lecturer begins by… Next… The lecturer concludes by… Again…

Weak Response

p.121

Evaluation

Score	5	4	3	2	1
Development			V		
Organization				V	
Unity				V	
Language Use			V		

Notes

This level-3 response frames the issues well. It discusses the points made in the listening and reading about green consumerism in somewhat unclear and error-prone language ("He says that the befits of green products have a hidden cost, which mean that there more benefits outweights the advantages"). In addition, the third point wrongly attributes one of the arguments from the reading to the listening ("Lastly, the listening talked about the green consumerism domino effect"). For these reasons, this response earns a 3.

Final Score: 3

Critical Analysis

Ⓐ

Answer Ⓐ is the best choice because it most accurately expresses the idea of the highlighted sentence. Answer Ⓑ goes against the argument presented in the lecture while Answer Ⓒ is not mentioned.

Spending Money on International Issues

◉ Generating Ideas
p.122

▷ **Agree**

Reason 1: *By spending money on international issues, rich nations can develop closer relationships with developing nations.*

Reason 2: *When rich nations give money to poorer nations, both the poorer nations and the rich nations can ultimately benefit.*

Reason 3: *If problems in less developed nations go unchecked, they can spread and become more severe.*

▷ **Disagree**

Reason 1: *Nations have an obligation to treat the problems of their own citizens first.*

Reason 2: *Donated money could be used by the leaders of other countries for purposes other than originally intended.*

Reason 3: *Rich nations might have other motives for giving assistance, such as forcing other nations to adopt specific policies or creating new trading partners.*

◉ Planning
p.123

Thesis Statement (Agree / Disagree)

I agree with the statement that the governments of rich nations should spend money on international issues rather than on domestic problems.

First Supporting Idea

First, donations from rich nations can prevent international issues from spreading and becoming more serious.

Supporting Example

To illustrate, consider the food shortages in North Korea.

Second Supporting Idea

Second, aid from rich nations can help make all nations of the world prosperous.

Supporting Example

As poorer nations gain economic prowess, they become important trading partners with the nations that provided them aid.

Third Supporting Idea

Finally, by spending money on international issues, rich nations can bring about global stability and promote world peace.

Supporting Example

This financial generosity has allowed the U.S. to gain allies in virtually every corner of the globe, therefore enabling the U.S. to maintain global stability.

Conclusion

But for the reasons given above, it is clear that rich nations should spend money on international issues rather than on domestic problems.

Strong Response
p.125

Critical Analysis

1 Therefore, I agree with the statement that the governments of rich nations should spend money on international issues rather than on domestic problems. / First, donations from rich nations can prevent international issues from spreading and becoming more serious. / In addition to preventing problems from spreading, aid from rich nations can help make all nations of the world prosperous. / But for the reasons given above, it is clear that rich nations should spend money on international issues rather than on domestic problems.

2 When rich nations provided aid, the North Korean people were able to subsist. / However, now that international aid has been cut off, thousands of North Koreans have been dying from starvation. / Rich nations must assist poorer nations in developing infrastructure and improving living standards for their citizens. / As poorer nations gain economic prowess, they become important trading partners with the nations that provided them aid. / This allows richer nations to develop their own economies while helping the people of less developed nations become wealthy.

3 food shortages in North Korea; poor nations becoming trading partners with rich nations; the United States and its allies throughout the world

Weak Response
p.127

Evaluation

Score	5	4	3	2	1
Development			V		
Organization			V		
Unity			V		
Language Use				V	

Notes

At first glance, this essay has the appearance of a strong

response. The paragraphs are reasonably well organized and generally flow smoothly. The two main issues keeping this response from scoring higher are its lack of clarity and development, which are caused by weak language use. This is most acutely seen in the second body paragraph, where most of the sentences, including the topic sentence ("Next giving too much money to other govermnets can revolt to the people") are extremely unclear.

Final Score: __3__

Critical Analysis

Ⓑ

Answer Ⓑ would best support the passage. Although the response discusses money, it does not mention taxation, making Answer Ⓐ incorrect. And while the response mentions citizens becoming unhappy, the situation is not similar enough to the American and French revolutions to use them as examples, making Answer Ⓒ also incorrect.

Chapter **07** | Integrated Writing

Business: Maintaining U.S. Policies Abroad

◊ Note-Taking   p.131

1 Main Idea of the Passage: *American companies should adopt American policies at their overseas affiliates.*

2 First Supporting Argument: *Following American policies would increase safety.*

3 Second Supporting Argument: *Enforcing an American code of ethics would provide employees with better working conditions.*

4 Third Supporting Argument: *Companies can improve their business by enforcing American work standards.*

Critical Thinking

1 Following American policies might be more expensive than following the local policies of a country, so it would reduce the company's profit margin.

2 No, I do not think so because some people might disagree with or even resent certain American policies.

◊ Listening   p.132

Script **02-07**

Professor: Now, let's talk a bit about American companies that open operations abroad. You know, many criticize these companies for failing to require their international subsidiaries to adopt American

policies, but I've always believed that when in Rome, do as the Romans do.

First, by not following local policies, these companies are, you know, losing tremendous business opportunities and hampering their competitiveness. For example, consider the case of the cell phone company that could not release its products in China because it, uh, failed to adhere to the government's policies preventing the use of Bluetooth technology. Because of this unwillingness to comply with local standards, the company lost tens of millions of dollars in potential revenue.

And speaking of following local customs, many American companies need to pay wages that are, um, in step with the local job market. To illustrate, American car companies paid their employees in Mexico double the legally mandated minimum wage because, from an American perspective, it was too low. As a result of this, the companies were unable to match the profit margins of other firms and ultimately had to move their operations to places where wages were even lower. In short, these companies had to fire all of their Mexican employees because they wanted to pay them higher wages.

On top of this is the issue of American ethical imperialism. What I mean is that by imposing American work standards onto their overseas affiliates, these companies are, um, alienating their foreign workforce and client base. To illustrate, one semiconductor manufacturer recently baffled and offended its foreign managers by requiring them to participate in a sexual harassment course. Indeed, many have long criticized this practice of forcing America cultural norms on others because they, um, often clash with the cultural values of the host country.

◊ Note-Taking   p.133

1 Main Idea of the Lecture: *American companies should adopt local customs when doing business internationally.*

2 First Supporting Argument: *Companies lose business opportunities by not following local policies.*

3 Second Supporting Argument: *American companies should pay wages appropriate for the local market.*

4 Third Supporting Argument: *Imposing an American code of ethics on foreign subsidiaries might alienate the foreign workforce and client base.*

Critical Thinking

1 The lecturer argues that following American policies

reduces a company's competitiveness, that paying American wages can force a foreign affiliate to go out of business, and that forcing others to follow American polices can damage business relationships.

2 The lecturer fails to address the increases in safety and improvements to a company's reputation brought about by following American policies.

◈ Tandem Note-Taking

p.134

Reading	Listening
Main Idea	**Main Idea**
American companies should adopt American policies at their overseas affiliates.	American companies should adopt local customs when doing business internationally.
First Supporting Argument	**First Supporting Argument**
Following American policies would increase safety.	Companies lose business opportunities by not following local policies.
Supporting Detail	**Supporting Detail**
Bhopal, India, accident	cell phone company could not release phones; did not comply with Chinese policies
Second Supporting Argument	
Enforcing an American code of ethics would provide employees with better working conditions.	**Second Supporting Argument**
	American companies should pay wages appropriate for the local market.
Supporting Detail	
outlaw child labor	**Supporting Detail**
Third Supporting Argument	American company paid Mexican workers high wages; could not compete
Companies can improve their business by enforcing American work standards.	**Third Supporting Argument**
Supporting Detail	Imposing an American code of ethics on foreign subsidiaries might alienate the foreign workforce and client base.
shoe company boycott; adopted American policies	
	Supporting Detail
	managers offended by sexual harassment course

Strong Response　p.136

Critical Analysis

1 While the reading supports adopting American policies, the lecturer strongly opposes it. / The professor begins by arguing that following American policies reduces the competitiveness of a company. / The lecturer then argues that companies lose business by following American policies. / The instructor concludes by arguing that companies that impose American work standards on foreign subsidiaries can alienate their foreign workforce and potential client base.

2 This is illustrated by a cell phone company that was unable to release its products in China because it refused to comply with Chinese policies, so it therefore lost millions of dollars in potential revenue. / For example, one car company paid its Mexican workers the American minimum wage rather than the local minimum wage. / By doing this, the company was not able to compete with other manufacturers and consequently had to move its production facilities elsewhere. / This is explained with the case of an American company that offended its foreign staff by requiring them to take a course on sexual harassment.

3 The professor begins by... The lecturer then argues... The instructor concludes by...

Weak Response　p.137

Evaluation

Score	5	4	3	2	1
Development		V			
Organization		V			
Unity	V				
Language Use		V			

Notes

This response does many things well. First, it generally does a good job of contrasting points from the reading passage and lecture. The response is also fairly well organized, especially in the second and third body paragraphs. This is bolstered by the fact that the response reads smoothly and includes clear connections between its ideas. What keeps this out of the level-5 range is the slight lack of development (especially the first body paragraph), which makes it difficult to fully understand the relationship between the reading passage and the lecture, coupled with the minor but somewhat frequent grammatical errors.

Final Score:　4

Answer Ⓐ is the best choice because it most accurately expresses the relationship between the first arguments presented in the reading passage and the lecture. Answers Ⓑ and Ⓒ are not directly stated in either the reading passage or the lecture.

Class Attendance Should Not Be Required

◈ Generating Ideas
p.138

▷ **Agree:**

Reason 1: *Making class attendance optional forces students to become independent, self-motivated workers.*

Reason 2: *Learning is assessed based solely on one or two major tests; for this reason, class attendance should be optional.*

Reason 3: *At university, students have access to textbooks, millions of library books, academic databases, and professors to help them with their studies.*

▷ **Disagree:**

Reason 1: *Mandatory class attendance can make learning more organized and help students focus on their studies.*

Reason 2: *By having only one assignment, students have only one chance to do well and have no opportunities to improve their performance.*

Reason 3: *Going to class is like going to work, so in this regard, mandatory class attendance prepares students to become employees with a set schedule.*

◈ Planning
p.139

Thesis Statement (Agree / Disagree)

I believe that class attendance should be mandatory even for university students because it provides a more structured learning environment, makes the grading process more equitable, and prepares students better for the working world.

First Supporting Idea

By making class attendance mandatory, students receive a superior education in a more structured learning environment.

Supporting Example

Students can study more efficiently.

Second Supporting Idea

In conjunction with making studying more structured, mandatory class attendance also makes the grading process more equitable.

Supporting Example

Having many assignments allows students to improve over the semester.

Third Supporting Idea

Class attendance can help prepare students for the working world.

Supporting Example

Going to class is similar to going to the office.

Conclusion

While a minority of students may flourish in a university environment in which class attendance is not mandatory, for the reasons I listed above, I feel that the majority of students learn best when they are required to go to class.

p.141

1 I believe that class attendance should be mandatory even for university students because it provides a more structured learning environment, makes the grading process more equitable, and prepares students better for the working world. / By making class attendance mandatory, students receive a superior education in a more structured learning environment. / In conjunction with making studying more structured, mandatory class attendance also makes the grading process more equitable. / To this end, mandatory class attendance is unquestionably pertinent.

2 University professors are experts in their fields and are therefore able to provide insight into subjects that students might not be able to glean themselves. / Furthermore, as many university students are still fairly immature, mandatory class attendance can help them remain focused on their studies while providing them with a study plan to make learning possible. / Students would have only one opportunity to demonstrate their learning, and if they did not study properly, they would fail the class. / However, mandatory class attendance allows students to test their knowledge at various intervals over the course of a semester and make changes to their study habits as needed. / Very few jobs allot employees, especially recent graduates, the freedom and the flexibility to work wherever and whenever they want. / When the students become employees, they will be expected to work regular hours according to a strict

schedule.

3 professors are experts; university students need structure; many assignments can help students perform better; class attendance is similar to work attendance

Weak Response p.143

Evaluation

Score	5	4	3	2	1
Development			V		
Organization			V		
Unity				V	
Language Use				V	

Notes

This response is at level 3. On the positive side, the response is reasonably well developed, and the organization is fairly good with each paragraph staying on topic. Additionally, the sentence structure is somewhat varied throughout the response. What prevents this essay from scoring high is a lack of unity, especially in the second body paragraph ("which means that even if you don't go to the leckture, you can still know what they have to teach, like the english teacher hwo puts the notes up online and then the study guide"). Some of the grammar and the syntax also obscure the meanings of some sentences. Overall, this is a solid essay that could be much better with a few important changes.

Final Score: ___3___

Critical Analysis

Ⓒ

Answer Ⓒ is the best choice because body paragraphs 1 and 2 both address the issue of studying outside of class. The content of body paragraph 3 cannot be joined with the content in the other body paragraphs, making Answers Ⓐ and Ⓑ incorrect.

Computer Science: Are Internet Encyclopedias Better?

◈ Note-Taking p.147

1 Main Idea of the Passage: *Traditional encyclopedias offer important advantages over online encyclopedias.*

2 First Supporting Argument: *Traditional encyclopedias are more accurate than online encyclopedias.*

3 Second Supporting Argument: *Traditional encyclopedias offer greater security than online encyclopedias.*

4 Third Supporting Argument: *Traditional encyclopedias contain only relevant information.*

Critical Thinking

1 Because virtually anyone can edit online encyclopedias, new information can be added easily, and errors can be corrected quickly.

2 I think online encyclopedias cover a wider variety of topics because anyone can contribute to them, which means that their personal interests can be included.

◈ Listening p.148

Script 02-08

Professor: With the rising popularity of Internet encyclopedias, traditional encyclopedias may soon become relics of the past. This should come as no surprise to anyone who has used both.

One supposed benefit of traditional encyclopedias is the fact that they contain fewer errors. While this may be the case, online encyclopedias have an advantage of their own that counters this: changeability. You see, because only a select group of people edit hardcover encyclopedias, errors in them can sometimes stay unchecked for years or even decades. But with online encyclopedias, this simply isn't a problem. Errors can be corrected immediately, ensuring that inaccurate information gets removed quickly.

In addition, Internet encyclopedias have their own safeguards that protect them from the spread of harmful misinformation. The reason is that online encyclopedias have groups of dedicated fact checkers—most of whom are professors and other scholars—who make sure that the information in the articles is as accurate as possible. Material that is incorrect or lacks citations may be challenged and removed if no outside supporting information is found. And do you know what else? Online encyclopedias utilize powerful encryption that cannot be easily hacked. In other words, the threat of data corruption and deletion by hackers is minimal.

And, oh . . . online encyclopedias contain a greater amount of information about a wider variety of topics. This is actually one of the strengths of a communal online encyclopedia. Readers can, um, delve into many different aspects of virtually any subject of interest. Topics as varied as blockbuster films and bestselling video games to subway systems and school bus engine design are all covered in online encyclopedias.

◈ Note-Taking

p.149

1 Main Idea of the Lecture: *Online encyclopedias will make traditional encyclopedias outdated.*

2 First Supporting Argument: *Online encyclopedias can be edited easily.*

3 Second Supporting Argument: *Online encyclopedias have security measures to protect their data.*

4 Third Supporting Argument: *Online encyclopedias cover a wider variety of topics.*

⬭ Critical Thinking

1 The professor refutes the idea that online encyclopedias contain incorrect information and that online encyclopedias include only trivial information.

2 The professor concedes that online encyclopedias may contain more errors than traditional encyclopedias but says the fact that Internet encyclopedias can be edited easily makes up for this fact.

◈ Tandem Note-Taking

p.150

Reading	Listening
Main Idea	**Main Idea**
Traditional encyclopedias offer important advantages over online encyclopedias.	*Online encyclopedias will make traditional encyclopedias outdated.*
First Supporting Argument	**First Supporting Argument**
Traditional encyclopedias are more accurate than online encyclopedias.	*Online encyclopedias can be edited easily.*
Supporting Detail	**Supporting Detail**
traditional encyclopedias fact-checked by scholars	*online encyclopedias errors quickly changed*
Second Supporting Argument	**Second Supporting Argument**
Traditional encyclopedias offer greater security than online encyclopedias.	*Online encyclopedias have security measures to protect their data.*
Supporting Detail	**Supporting Detail**
cannot alter traditional encyclopedias	*fact checkers for online encyclopedias; challenge and remove inaccuracies*
Third Supporting Argument	**Third Supporting Argument**
Traditional encyclopedias contain only relevant information.	*Online encyclopedias cover a wider variety of topics.*
Supporting Detail	**Supporting Detail**
authors are scholars; know important information	*research virtually any topic*

Strong Response

p.152

Critical Analysis

1 His argument that Internet encyclopedias are superior to traditional encyclopedias contradicts the reading passage's claim that traditional encyclopedias are superior to online ones. / The lecturer explains that while online encyclopedias may have more errors than hardbound texts, they have their own advantage of changeability. / The professor goes on to explain that Internet encyclopedias have safeguards to prevent the spread of misinformation. / The instructor contends that the wider variety of topics covered in online encyclopedias is one of their greatest strengths over hardbound encyclopedias.

2 He contends that because traditional encyclopedias are only edited by a small number of people, errors contained in them can go unchecked for several

years. / He contrasts this with Internet encyclopedias. / Because they can be edited immediately, their errors get removed quickly. / He illustrates this by mentioning that online encyclopedias have fact checkers who delete information in articles that is inaccurate or otherwise not correct. / He also mentions that online encyclopedias have powerful encryption to stop the threat of hackers corrupting the site. / He explains that readers can research virtually any subject that interests them, including famous video games and subways.

3 First of all… The professor goes on to explain… He also mentions… Lastly…

Weak Response

Evaluation

Score	5	4	3	2	1
Development		V			
Organization	V				
Unity		V			
Language Use			V		

Notes

This level-4 response includes all the arguments from the passage and the lecture, and it explains how their arguments oppose one another. What keeps this response from scoring higher are some lapses in clarity ("paragraph said that traditionel encyclopedia present the pertenent information only, unlike the in the lecture, that said online encyclopedias that have many differ subjects") and a lack of development (the third paragraph does not include any examples from the lecture). Overall, this response falls near the bottom of the level 4 range.

Final Score: 4

Critical Analysis

Answer Ⓒ is the best choice because it would help develop the final paragraph by including some examples from the lecture. Answer Ⓑ is not directly mentioned in either the reading passage or the lecture. And while Answer Ⓐ is attractive, a detailed explanation is not necessary to complete this task.

Chapter 08 | Independent Writing

Documentaries and Books

◈ Generating Ideas

▷ **Agree**

Reason 1: *People like documentaries because they are short yet contain a lot of information about a certain topic.*

Reason 2: *Documentaries show videos and graphics, which help people who are visually oriented. This allows certain people to learn better than they would from reading books.*

Reason 3: *Many people have short attention spans, so they cannot read long books. Other people also do not like reading but enjoy watching videos, so documentaries are appropriate for them.*

▷ **Disagree**

Reason 1: *Books can contain much more information than documentaries can because books are long while documentaries are short.*

Reason 2: *Documentaries are made to entertain people whereas books are written to educate people.*

Reason 3: *Books can be written for people of different age levels, so they use appropriate words and expressions, which makes them easy to understand.*

◈ Planning

Thesis Statement (Agree / Disagree)

There is no way anyone can learn as much from watching documentaries as they can from reading books for a wide variety of reasons.

First Supporting Idea

Books contain so much more information than documentaries do.

Supporting Example

documentary on volcano had small amount of information; book contained much more information

Second Supporting Idea

Authors write their books with the objective of getting their readers to learn whereas documentary makers are primarily trying to entertain their audience.

Supporting Example

documentaries are well produced and have great graphics but don't learn from them; books are written to educate people

Third Supporting Idea

Many books are written at a high level while

documentaries are often made with children in mind.

Supporting Example

saw documentary for kids so no new information; books available for people of all learning levels.

Conclusion

For the reasons outlined above, this improved access to information has made life better for virtually everybody.

Strong Response   p.157

Critical Analysis

1 There is no way anyone can learn as much from watching documentaries as they can from reading books for a wide variety of reasons. / The first reason that I disagree is that books contain so much more information than documentaries do. / The second reason that I disagree is that authors write their books with the objective of getting their readers to learn whereas documentary makers are primarily trying to entertain their audience. / The third reason that I disagree is that many books are written at a high level while documentaries are often made with children in mind. / It is obvious that books are more educational than documentary.

2 Recently, I watched a documentary about volcanoes. / It was pretty interesting, and it was based on a book that had been published. / However, the documentary only lasted for an hour. / I went to the library and checked out the book the documentary was based on. / I simply could not believe how much information the book contained. / The documentary had only covered a small amount of information. / I learned so much more from the book than I did from the documentary. / I have seen plenty of documentaries on space. / They are usually well produced and have great graphics, but I almost never learn from them despite the fact that they look good. / I have also read many books on space. / For example, I saw a documentary on lions last week. / It was for kids, so it contained no information that I did not already know. / On the other hand, there are books that are available for people of all learning levels. / There are books for elementary school children, high schoolers, college students, and adults.

3 checking out book; seeing documentaries on space; not learning from them; reading books written to educate people; seeing documentary on lions; not learning because was for kids; learning from books for appropriate ages

---

Weak Response   p.159

Evaluation

Score	5	4	3	2	1
Development					V
Organization					V
Unity					V
Language Use				V	

Notes

This response uses good grammar and many correct words and appears to provide a lot of information. However, the essay does not actually answer the question, which tells respondents to agree or disagree with the statement. Instead, the writer focuses on the benefits of both documentaries and books. The response is basically about the writer's personal life, which is not relevant to the question. This essay fails to respond to the question, so it earns a score of 1.

Final Score: 1

Critical Analysis

Ⓒ

Answer Ⓒ is the correct choice because it best explains this response's shortcomings. Answer Ⓐ is incorrect because the language and the grammar are fine while Answer Ⓑ is not correct because the writer provides several personal examples.

Chapter **09** | Integrated Writing

Archaeology: Is the Sphinx Actually Ancient?

◈ **Note-Taking**   p.163

1 Main Idea of the Passage: *The Sphinx was constructed during the Old Kingdom.*

2 First Supporting Argument: *The Sphinx's facial features date it to the Old Kingdom.*

3 Second Supporting Argument: *The tombstone at the base of the Sphinx explains the statue's history.*

4 Third Supporting Argument: *The erosion on the Sphinx also dates it to the Old Kingdom.*

Critical Thinking

1 *The current appearance might not be the original appearance. Perhaps the sculpture was damaged in the past and was rebuilt using the Old Kingdom style.*

2 *No, I do not feel this is good evidence because the tombstone could have been added later while the story on it might have been made up.*

Script 02-09

Professor: Um, a lot of scholarly time and energy has been spent trying to solve the so-called "Riddle of the Sphinx." Although many attribute the Sphinx to the Old Kingdom Era, new evidence suggests that the monument may be more ancient than was previously thought.

Okay, so one of the arguments in favor of the Old Kingdom theory is about the structure of the Sphinx's face. Well, as it turns out, the current head on the Sphinx may not be the original one. Archaeologists have recently discovered hieroglyphs depicting the Sphinx with the head of a lion, not the human head we see today. Moreover, the current head is, uh, disproportionately small for the body. So it's quite probable that the original head became damaged, and a new head was later sculpted out of the leftover rock.

Another favorite piece of evidence you may have heard about is the tombstone in front of the statue. As it turns out, the tombstone was not built at the same time as the Sphinx but was made several centuries later during the New Kingdom. In fact, researchers believe that the Pharaoh Thutmose created the tombstone and its legend as a way to justify his, um, ascension to the throne. That is to say, the story on the tombstone is probably more fiction than fact.

And, uh, one more thing I'd like to talk about is the erosion on the statue. The weathering on the Sphinx was most likely caused by extended periods of heavy rain. But according to archaeological evidence, Egypt has averaged less than one inch of rainfall annually for the past four thousand years, so the erosion on the Sphinx must have happened prior to the Old Kingdom. This is backed up by meteorological evidence showing that Egypt's last period of significant rainfall occurred more than five millennia ago.

◈ **Note-Taking** p.165

1 Main Idea of the Lecture: *Evidence suggests that the Sphinx might be older than was previously thought.*

2 First Supporting Argument: *The current face on the Sphinx may not be the original one.*

3 Second Supporting Argument: *The tombstone was built much later than the Sphinx.*

4 Third Supporting Argument: *The erosion on the Sphinx occurred prior to the Old Kingdom.*

Critical Thinking

1 *The professor argues that the current face was not the original one. She also says that the tombstone was added several centuries after the Sphinx was built and that the erosion on the Sphinx occurred before the Old Kingdom.*

2 *She mentions that the Sphinx originally had a lion's head. She also explains that the tombstone was built centuries after the Sphinx was constructed. Finally, she says that the last period of heavy rainfall in Egypt occurred prior to the Old Kingdom.*

◈ **Tandem Note-Taking** p.166

Reading	Listening
Main Idea *The Sphinx was constructed during the Old Kingdom.*	**Main Idea** *Evidence suggests that the Sphinx might be older than was previously thought.*
First Supporting Argument *The Sphinx's facial features date it to the Old Kingdom.*	**First Supporting Argument** *The current face on the Sphinx may not be the original one.*
Supporting Detail *Sphinx headdress like other Old Kingdom statues*	**Supporting Detail** *originally lion's head*
Second Supporting Argument *The tombstone at the base of the Sphinx explains the statue's history.*	**Second Supporting Argument** *The tombstone was built much later than the Sphinx.*
Supporting Detail *Sphinx Old Kingdom guardian angel*	**Supporting Detail** *tombstone added later by pharaoh; justified his rule*
Third Supporting Argument *The erosion on the Sphinx also dates it to the Old Kingdom.*	**Third Supporting Argument** *The erosion on the Sphinx occurred prior to the Old Kingdom.*
Supporting Detail *erosion similar to Old Kingdom pyramids*	**Supporting Detail** *erosion occurred before Old Kingdom*

Strong Response p.168

Critical Analysis

1 Her arguments cast doubt on the claims made in the

reading passage. / First, the instructor talks about the history of the Sphinx's face. / Next, the lecturer explains the history of the tombstone at the front of the Sphinx. / Finally, the professor discusses the erosion on the Sphinx.

2   She explains that the current face on the Sphinx may be a later reconstruction due to the fact that archaeologists have discovered hieroglyphs showing the Sphinx with a lion's head. / She says that the stone was actually built several centuries after the Sphinx. / Furthermore, the legend depicted on the stone was created by a later pharaoh to justify his ascension to the throne. / She mentions that the weathering on the statue is the result of heavy rainfall and concludes that the Sphinx must have been constructed during the Early Dynastic Period.

3   First… Next… Furthermore… Finally…

Weak Response
p.169

Evaluation

Score	5	4	3	2	1
Development				V	
Organization			V		
Unity			V		
Language Use			V		

Notes

This response includes most of the information from both the reading and the listening. However, the third body paragraph incorrectly labels the information from the reading passage and the lecture. The response also suffers from a lack of development, especially in the third body paragraph. This is compounded by weak organization that makes the response difficult to follow. The grammatical problems and the use of only short, simple sentences further contribute to these weaknesses, earning this response a score of 3.

Final Score: __3__

Critical Analysis

Ⓑ

Answer Ⓑ is the best choice. Although the response mentions the heavy rainfall, it does not explain when the rainfall occurred, which is the central idea of the argument in the lecture. Answer Ⓐ is incorrect because the response explains that the original head might have been a lion. Answer Ⓒ is also explained, although in unclear language, in the response.

Reading a Book a Second Time Is More Interesting

◊ Generating Ideas
p.170

▷ **Agree**

Reason 1: *By understanding the basic plot of a novel, you are able to appreciate it more for its artistic qualities, such as the beauty of the writing.*

Reason 2: *Rereading a novel, especially a complex one, allows you to understand the relationships and personalities of the characters and how they relate to the overall narrative.*

Reason 3: *Certain scenes and beautiful writing can be appreciated over and over again.*

▷ **Disagree**

Reason 1: *Many novels, such as mystery novels, are mainly interesting because you do not know the outcome. By rereading such novels, the dramatic tension is gone.*

Reason 2: *Because you already know the characters and the outcome of the story, it can be difficult to stay interested in the novel, therefore making it more difficult to understand.*

Reason 3: *If you did not like a novel the first time, there is little reason to go back and read it again. There are also literally millions of novels in the world, so you should not waste any time rereading ones you have already read.*

◊ Planning
p.171

Thesis Statement (Agree / Disagree)
I agree with the statement that reading a book a second time is more interesting than reading it the first time.

First Supporting Idea
When I reread a novel, I can enjoy the story more.

Supporting Example
Some novels have dozens of characters, and the only way to understand the relationships between them is to read the novel again.

Second Supporting Idea
Rereading a novel also allows me to revisit my favorite parts of the story.

Supporting Example
Some scenes are especially exciting and fun to read.

Third Supporting Idea
Finally, by revisiting the novel, I am able to understand

the work more deeply.

Supporting Example
William Faulkner's works contain symbolism that is not obvious the first time you read it.

Conclusion
I believe it is much more enjoyable to read a novel a second time than it is the first time.

Strong Response
p.173

Critical Analysis

1 That is why I agree with the statement that reading a book a second time is more interesting than reading it the first time. / When I reread a novel, I can enjoy the story more. / Rereading a novel also allows me to revisit my favorite parts of the story. / Finally, by revisiting the novel, I am able to understand the work more deeply / All things considered, I believe it is much more enjoyable to read a novel a second time than it is the first time.

2 One such example is Leo Tolstoy's *War and Peace*, which contains dozens of characters, each with his or her own story arc. / The dialog between the men, with the villain making thinly veiled threats against the owner's life, is rife with dramatic tension. / Ostensibly a hunting narrative, the true purpose of the story is to explain the guilt the main character has about his lineage and the remorse he feels after slaying the bear, which represents man's destruction of nature.

3 the complex novel, *War and Peace*; the dramatic scene in *No Country for Old Men*; the symbolism in *The Bear*

Weak Response
p.175

Evaluation

Score	5	4	3	2	1
Development		V			
Organization		V			
Unity	V				
Language Use		V			

Notes

This response does many things well. It presents its arguments in an organized, fairly clear manner with each paragraph generally transitioning well between ideas. What prevents this essay from scoring higher is a slight lack of elaboration and some organizational issues. The response needs more development to support the writer's ideas,

and in terms of organization, the first and second body paragraphs essentially make the same argument (rereading a book is not exciting) and would be better combined into one paragraph. For these reasons, this essay earns a score of 4.

Final Score: ___4___

Critical Analysis

Ⓐ

Answer Ⓐ is the best choice because body paragraphs 1 and 2 both argue that rereading a novel is not exciting.

Chapter **10** | Integrated Writing

Chemistry: The Problems Caused by Sulfur Dioxide

◈ Note-Taking
p.179

1 Main Idea of the Passage: *Sulfur dioxide harms living creatures and the environment.*

2 First Supporting Argument: *Sulfur dioxide creates smog.*

3 Second Supporting Argument: *Sulfur dioxide produces acid rain.*

4 Third Supporting Argument: *Inhaling sulfur dioxide causes health problems.*

Critical Thinking

1 Yes, I think smog can sometimes be beneficial because it reduces the amount of sunlight that reaches the Earth's surface. This might help cool the Earth and prevent sun-related health problems.

2 The people who get sick from sulfur dioxide exposure are probably physically weak or already sick.

◈ Listening
p.180

Script 02-10

Professor: You know, you always hear about the negative effects of sulfur dioxide, so let's address a few points that most environmentalists seem to overlook. You might be surprised by what the research tells us.

So we all know that aerosols are harmful to the ozone layer and the environment, right? Well, it turns out that having at least some aerosols in the atmosphere is actually a good thing. You see, the aerosols produced by sulfur dioxide can be beneficial because they reflect sunlight back into space. This has the effect of cooling the Earth. In fact, studies have shown that decreasing sulfur dioxide emissions has led to regional warming in various parts of the world.

Then there is the issue of sulfur dioxide and acid rain. Although sulfur dioxide is often cited as a scapegoat, it is not the only chemical in acid rain. The nitrogen oxide and the carbon dioxide emitted from internal combustion engines are, um, largely responsible for producing acid rain. In actuality, sulfur dioxide is one of the least abundant chemicals in acid rain thanks to recent efforts to reduce sulfur dioxide levels.

Oh, one other thing I'd like to talk about is the health problems purportedly caused by sulfur dioxide. Sure, there are a few thousand documented cases of illnesses stemming from exposure to sulfur dioxide each year, but you have to consider that it usually affects only at-risk groups: infants, the elderly, and the terminally ill. Research shows that healthy people rarely become sick even after prolonged exposure to sulfur dioxide. What's more, other chemicals, including nitrogen oxide and carbon monoxide, are much more harmful than sulfur dioxide.

◈ Note-Taking
p.181

1 Main Idea of the Lecture: *Sulfur dioxide may not be as harmful as environmentalists suggest.*

2 First Supporting Argument: *The aerosols produced by sulfur dioxide can help cool the Earth.*

3 Second Supporting Argument: *Sulfur dioxide is not the only chemical in acid rain.*

4 Third Supporting Argument: *Sulfur dioxide only causes sickness in at-risk groups.*

Critical Thinking

1 The instructor refutes the idea that the smog produced by sulfur dioxide is completely harmful. He also rebuts the notion that sulfur dioxide is the most harmful substance in acid rain. Finally, the lecturer contradicts the reading passage's claim that exposure to sulfur dioxide can make anybody sick.

2 The instructor fails to rebut the arguments made against smog, acid rain, and the health problems created by sulfur dioxide. The lecturer seems to bring up additional points about sulfur dioxide rather than refute the arguments made in the reading.

◈ Tandem Note-Taking
p.182

Reading	Listening
Main Idea *Sulfur dioxide harms living creatures and the environment.*	**Main Idea** *Sulfur dioxide may not be as harmful as environmentalists suggest.*
First Supporting Argument *Sulfur dioxide creates smog.*	**First Supporting Argument** *The aerosols produced by sulfur dioxide can help cool the Earth.*
Supporting Detail *increases vehicular accidents; results in depression*	**Supporting Detail** *regional warming in some places*
Second Supporting Argument *Sulfur dioxide produces acid rain.*	**Second Supporting Argument** *Sulfur dioxide is not the only chemical in acid rain.*
Supporting Detail *destroys crops, pollutes water, damages buildings*	**Supporting Detail** *nitrogen oxide, carbon dioxide mostly in acid rain*
Third Supporting Argument *Inhaling sulfur dioxide causes health problems.*	**Third Supporting Argument** *Sulfur dioxide only causes sickness in at-risk groups.*
Supporting Detail *asthma, reparatory difficulties, emergency room visits, hospitalization*	**Supporting Detail** *at-risk groups get sick; infants, elderly, terminally ill*

Strong Response
p.184

Critical Analysis

1 By examining research that environmentalists tend to overlook, the lecturer argues that sulfur dioxide may not be as harmful as the reading passage suggests. / First of all, the lecturer mentions that having some aerosols in the atmosphere is beneficial. / The instructor also argues that sulfur dioxide is not one of the primary chemicals in acid rain. / Finally, the professor contends that sulfur dioxide is not seriously harmful to one's health.

2 He explains that the aerosols reflect sunlight back into space, which helps cool the Earth. / He illustrates this by saying that the reduction in sulfur dioxide emissions has led to warming in some parts of the world. / He says that acid rain is primarily caused by nitrogen oxide and carbon dioxide emitted from automobiles. / He argues that the people who get sick after being exposed to sulfur dioxide are in at-

risk groups, such as infants and the elderly. / He goes on to explain that sulfur dioxide rarely makes healthy people sick and that other chemicals, such as carbon monoxide, are much more harmful.

3 First of all… The lecturer also argues… Finally… He goes on to explain…

p.185
Weak Response

Evaluation

Score	5	4	3	2	1
Development				V	
Organization				V	
Unity				V	
Language Use				V	

Notes

This response includes most of the information from the reading and listening, but it has many weaknesses holding it back. For one, it relies on a block format, which makes a direct comparison between the reading and the listening difficult. Next, it misrepresents some points from the lecture ("Secondly, sulfer dioxide can not make the acid rain, unlike nitragen dioxide"). Finally, the poor grammar makes it difficult to understand what the writer is trying to convey. For these reasons, this response earns a 2.

Final Score: 2

Critical Analysis

 A

Answer Ⓐ is the correct choice because the response states that healthy people sometimes become sick due to exposure to sulfur dioxide while the lecturer says it only affects at-risk groups.

Chapter 10 | Independent Writing
Higher Education Is Only for Good Students

Generating Ideas
p.186

▷ **Agree**

Reason 1: *They do not admit all applicants because they want students who are capable of learning and working at a high level.*

Reason 2: *Allowing only good students into higher education institutions can have a positive effect because all of the students will be hard working and interested in their studies.*

Reason 3: *Good students can learn more effectively and are more likely to use the information they learn after graduation.*

▷ **Disagree**

Reason 1: *Weaker students can more greatly benefit because they have more room for improvement as a result of higher education.*

Reason 2: *Society benefits in many ways when a greater number of people are more educated since they are more likely to be socially aware and racially tolerant.*

Reason 3: *Non-academic areas such as sports teams and social clubs may deteriorate from a lack of student diversity.*

Planning
p.187

Thesis Statement (Agree / Disagree)
Not just good students should have access to higher education.

First Supporting Idea
There are many kinds of schools for many kinds of students.

Supporting Example
There are technical schools, vocational schools, community colleges, and many others.

Second Supporting Idea
Higher education can allow weaker students to grow academically.

Supporting Example
There is the story of my friend who barely made it to college and is now getting a master's degree.

Third Supporting Idea
Having a greater number of educated people benefits society.

Supporting Example
Educated people are more likely to vote and to volunteer in their communities.

Conclusion
Higher education should be available to all students.

p.189
Strong Response

Critical Analysis

1 I disagree with the statement that only good students should have access to higher education. / One of the strongest arguments in favor of allowing more

students to have access to higher education is the many different types of schools that exist. / Allowing weaker students to obtain a higher education allows them to grow academically. / For the reasons illustrated above, it is clear that higher education should be available to all students.

2 But during the twentieth century, new types of higher education institutions, such as community colleges and vocational schools, were developed with the aim of preparing students for the workforce rather than a career in academics. / Although universities denied him entry, he was able to matriculate into a community college. / There, he developed an interest in history and began taking his studies seriously. / His grades improved dramatically, and after two years, he was able to transfer to a four-year university. / Today, he is getting his master's degree at one of the most prestigious universities in the country.

3 different types of higher education institutions; the story of a friend who barely made it into college but is now getting a master's degree

Weak Response   p.191

Evaluation

Score	5	4	3	2	1
Development			V		
Organization			V		
Unity			V		
Language Use				V	

Notes

This response has many solid characteristics but is weakened by a few serious drawbacks. On the positive side, it is fairly well organized with each body paragraph focused on one idea. It also includes a reasonable amount of development with the example about the Ivy League schools being the best developed. Unfortunately, this response is held back by a lack of clarity (the second body paragraph in particular is not clearly written) resulting in large part from poor grammar and strange word choices. With stronger grammar and a better second body paragraph, this response could have easily scored higher.

Final Score: ___3___

Critical Analysis

Ⓑ

Answer Ⓑ is the correct choice because it best supports the response's central idea. Answer Ⓐ runs contrary to the central idea, and Answer Ⓒ does not specifically support the thesis of the response.

Zoology: The Purpose of Zebra Stripes

◈ Note-Taking   p.195

1 Main Idea of the Passage: *The zebra's stripes protect it from predators.*

2 First Supporting Argument: *The zebra's stripes create an optical illusion that tricks predators.*

3 Second Supporting Argument: *The zebra's stripes confuse predators.*

4 Third Supporting Argument: *The zebra's stripes camouflage the zebra.*

Critical Thinking

1 This suggests that their stripes may not adequately protect them from hunters, so they need to be able to escape quickly.

2 The stripes might help attract potential mates. They might also be purely for decoration.

◈ Listening   p.196

Script 02-11

Professor: Hmm, so we all know about zebras and their unique stripes, but what we don't know is why they have them. Even after examining zoological studies, the purpose of the stripes remains unclear.

Stripes may alter the zebra's appearance, but it turns out that they are ineffectual as a way to protect the zebra from imminent predator attacks . . . They don't alert the zebra to potential dangers. The reason is that most of the zebra's predators do not rely on the leaping method to attack. Instead, these hunters usually chase the zebra across a plain, so they rely on their superior stamina to catch their prey. Once the zebra finally succumbs to fatigue, the predator then goes in for the kill.

Another thing that you have to consider is the fact that predators are not confused by the stripes—not anymore, at least. Zoologists have observed lions chasing herds of zebras in the wild. What they found was that the lions were rarely thrown off by the zebra's coloration. What's more, they compared this data to data from other lion hunts. Can you guess what they discovered . . . ? That's right. Lions were able to hunt zebras as effectively as they hunted animals with mono-colored bodies.

Perhaps the most confounding piece of evidence is the fact that hiding is not really a part of a zebra's behavior. It turns out that zebras generally prefer to stay in open plains. This has both negative and positive effects for the zebra. On the one hand, the zebras are in plain sight . . . They can easily be seen by hunters. But at the same time, the zebras can spot potential threats from far away. So really, zebras prefer to stay out in the open in order to take preemptive action to escape from possible attacks.

◈ Note-Taking

p.197

1 Main Idea of the Lecture: *The purpose of the zebra's stripes is unclear.*

2 First Supporting Argument: *The zebra's stripes do not warn the zebras of predator attacks.*

3 Second Supporting Argument: *The stripes do not confuse predators anymore.*

4 Third Supporting Argument: *Zebras generally do not hide from predators.*

(Critical Thinking)

1 The professor refutes the idea that the stripes trick predators into attacking prematurely. She also calls into question the argument that the zebra's stripes confuse predators. Finally, the instructor explains that zebras prefer to say out in the open rather than relying on their stripes to hide from predators.

2 She explains that most of the zebra's predators prefer to chase the zebra when they are hunting. She also describes how lions are not confused by the zebra's stripes and why the zebras prefer to stay in open plains.

◈ Tandem Note-Taking

p.198

Reading	Listening
Main Idea *The zebra's stripes protect it from predators.*	**Main Idea** *The purpose of the zebra's stripes is unclear.*
First Supporting Argument *The zebra's stripes create an optical illusion that tricks predators.*	**First Supporting Argument** *The zebra's stripes do not warn the zebras of predator attacks.*
Supporting Detail *stripes make zebra appear larger than really is*	**Supporting Detail** *predators do not use leaping method*
Second Supporting Argument *The zebra's stripes confuse predators.*	**Second Supporting Argument** *The stripes do not confuse predators anymore.*
Supporting Detail *is difficult to track individual zebras*	**Supporting Detail** *lions not confused by zebra stripes*
Third Supporting Argument *The zebra's stripes camouflage the zebra.*	**Third Supporting Argument** *Zebras generally do not hide from predators.*
Supporting Detail *can hide in tall grass*	**Supporting Detail** *prefer staying in open plains*

Strong Response

p.200

(Critical Analysis)

1 This contradicts the passage's claim that the stripes protect the zebra from predators. / The professor begins by stating that stripes do not warn the zebra of predator attacks. / Next, the lecturer mentions that the stripes do not confuse predators. / Finally, the instructor explains that zebras generally do not hide.

2 The lecturer explains that the reason is that most of the zebra's predators do not use the leaping method to attack but instead chase the zebra across plains. / This is supported by the findings of zoologists, who found that lions were rarely confused by the zebra's stripes. / Moreover, the zoologists discovered that the lions were equally capable of hunting both zebras and mono-colored animals. / The lecturer explains that they usually stay in open plains where they can spot predators from far away.

3 The professor begins by… Next… Moreover… Finally…

Evaluation

Score	5	4	3	2	1
Development			V		
Organization			V		
Unity				V	
Language Use			V		

Notes

This response's strengths are that it includes most of the information, including some supporting ideas, from the lecture. It also has fairly strong organization with each body paragraph focusing on one of the main points from the listening. What keeps this essay from scoring higher is its lack of unity, namely the weak connections between sentences. It is also held back by the fact that the third body paragraph is so poorly written that it fails to convey information clearly, especially its topic sentence ("Thirdly, the zebra like to stay in open planes and the strips do not assist because of the plane sight. This means that the zebra easily sees prediters themselves"). For these reasons, this response scores a 3.

Final Score: __3__

Critical Analysis

Answer Ⓒ is the best choice because the third body paragraph does not explain which information comes from the reading passage and which information comes from the lecture.

Chapter **11** | Independent Writing

Art Galleries and Musical Performances vs. Sports Facilities

◈ Generating Ideas   p.202

▷ **Agree**

Reason 1: *Art and music are both important to culture. They show how people think and how they experience life.*

Reason 2: *People can gain access to culture if the government supports art and music.*

Reason 3: *They go to art galleries to see art, and they visit concert halls to see musical performances.*

▷ **Disagree**

Reason 1: *People spend quality time with their friends and family members when they watch sports.*

Reason 2: *Many people are overweight and out of shape, so government support for sports can help people physically.*

Reason 3: *Sports teach people about teamwork and also help them get in shape.*

◈ Planning   p.203

Thesis Statement

In my opinion, the government should definitely spend money to support art galleries and musical performances rather than spend money to support sports facilities.

First Supporting Idea

Art galleries and musical performances are an important aspect of culture.

Supporting Example

Musical tradition goes back hundreds of years; need to see artwork produced by country's artists

Second Supporting Idea

It is not easy for people to become artists or musicians.

Supporting Example

Spend a great deal of money on lessons; musical instruments are expensive

Third Supporting Idea

There are plenty of places in my city for people to watch sporting events, yet there are few places for them to experience the arts.

Supporting Example

government should construct galleries and concert halls; great use of taxpayer funds.

Conclusion

The government should clearly prioritize art galleries and musical performances over sporting events.

Critical Analysis

1   In my opinion, the government should definitely spend money to support art galleries and musical performances rather than spend money to support sports facilities. / For starters, art galleries and musical performances are an important aspect of culture. / A second reason is that it is not easy for people to become artists or musicians. / Finally, there are plenty of places in my city for people to watch sporting events, yet there are few places for them to experience the arts. / The government should clearly prioritize art galleries and musical performances over

sporting events.

2 In my country, we have many famous artists. / We also have a musical tradition that goes back hundreds of years. / They have to spend a great amount of money on lessons when they are young. / In addition, musical instruments can cost thousands of dollars. / My brother was in his school band, and it cost my parents very much money to buy him a trumpet. / When people finally become artists or musicians, they do not make much money as well. / So they often lead difficult lives.

3 many famous artists; musical tradition that goes back hundreds of years; spend a great amount of money on lessons; musical instruments can cost thousands of dollars; spend money constructing galleries for displaying art; spend money to build concert halls

Weak Response
p.207

Evaluation

Score	5	4	3	2	1
Development		V			
Organization		V			
Unity			V		
Language Use				V	

Notes

This response has both positive and negative aspects. First, it is developed well as there are three solid arguments made. It is also organized well as each paragraph has supporting details. However, the language use in the essay is poor. The sentences are very short and simple. There are also a number of grammar mistakes that do not make the essay unreadable but do make it difficult to read and to understand. Overall, this is a level-3 response.

Final Score: 3

Critical Analysis

Answer (A) is the best choice because it supports the claim made in the passage that the government should spend more money on sports facilities. Answer (B) is not related to the argument made in the essay while Answer (C) is the opposite of the main idea of the essay.

Psychology: TV Addiction

◆ Note-Taking
p.211

1 Main Idea of the Passage: *Television addiction has many serious side effects.*

2 First Supporting Argument: *Heavy television watching causes symptoms similar to clinical gambling addiction.*

3 Second Supporting Argument: *Heavy viewers suffer from emotional problems.*

4 Third Supporting Argument: *Television addiction also affects family members and friends.*

Critical Thinking

1 The symptoms associated with heavy viewing are similar to those of video game players, film buffs, and those of many other activities that people enjoy.

2 The paragraph implies that heavy viewers suffer from emotional problems as a result of watching television, but the argument fails to prove this.

◆ Listening
p.212

Script 02-12

Professor: One of today's most heated debates surrounds watching television. While proponents of television addiction have many arguments, most of their ideas just don't hold water.

Of course, people spend a lot of time in front of the TV. But they do that because it's an enjoyable way to unwind during their free time. Since watching TV is a passive activity, your body and mind have the opportunity to get some much-needed rest. On top of that, watching television is a great way to reduce stress. Surprised? Researchers have found that watching television actually lowers your heart rate, allowing viewers to feel, um, peaceful and at ease. Additionally, these relaxing effects continue long after the set has been turned off.

Then there's the argument that television creates negative emotions. You know, whenever we are without something important to us—be it family, friends, or even television—we tend to feel anxious and lonely. So it's only natural that people crave television when they aren't around it. Moreover, researchers have yet to establish a, uh, correlation between prolonged television watching and depression. They, um . . . aren't sure which causes which. So really, the jury is still out about whether television causes people to feel lonely.

Finally, there seems to be confusion over the

word addiction. Whenever you read about so-called television addictions, the word is never clearly defined. The reason is that it has different meanings for the general public and psychologists. Most people use the word addiction quite loosely, but for psychologists, the word has a narrow meaning in a clinical context. And while most psychologists agree that some people spend too much time in front of the boob tube, there is, uh, no consensus that this is a serious problem.

◈ Note-Taking

p.213

1 Main Idea of the Lecture: *Television addiction is not a proven problem.*

2 First Supporting Argument: *Watching television is an enjoyable way to spend your free time.*

3 Second Supporting Argument: *People are naturally anxious whenever something they like is not around.*

4 Third Supporting Argument: *The word addiction has a different meaning for psychologists.*

Critical Thinking

1 The instructor refutes the idea that watching television is entirely unhealthy. She also argues that television does not necessarily cause negative emotions. Finally, she explains that people misuse the word addiction.

2 The instructor fails to address the problems specifically caused by prolonged periods of viewing. It also does not prove that television does not cause loneliness.

◈ Tandem Note-Taking

p.214

Reading	Listening
Main Idea *Television addiction has many serious side effects.*	**Main Idea** *Television addiction is not a proven problem.*
First Supporting Argument *Heavy television watching causes symptoms similar to clinical gambling addiction.*	**First Supporting Argument** *Watching television is an enjoyable way to spend your free time.*
Supporting Detail *cannot stop watching even though harmful*	**Supporting Detail** *helps you relax; reduces stress*
Second Supporting Argument *Heavy viewers suffer from emotional problems.*	**Second Supporting Argument** *People are naturally anxious whenever something they like is not around.*
Supporting Detail *suffer from withdrawal symptoms*	**Supporting Detail** *become lonely without family and friends*
Third Supporting Argument *Television addiction also affects family and friends.*	**Third Supporting Argument** *The word addiction has a different meaning for psychologists.*
Supporting Detail *physically and emotionally withdrawn*	**Supporting Detail** *limited, clinical meaning for psychologists*

Strong Response

p.216

Critical Analysis

1 Her arguments go against the ones presented in the reading passage. / First, the professor states that watching television is a good way to relax during your free time. / Next, the instructor explains that people naturally feel anxious and lonely whenever something they crave is not around, be it television or family and friends. / Finally, the lecturer delves into the confusion over the word addiction.

2 Because watching television is a passive activity, your body and mind are able to rest. / Furthermore, watching television can reduce stress because it lowers your heart rate. / Additionally, researchers have yet to establish a correlation between television watching and depression. / For the general public, the word addiction has a broad meaning while for psychologists, it has a narrow clinical meaning. / The professor also mentions that psychologists have

yet to reach a consensus about whether prolonged television viewing has serious consequences.

3 First… Furthermore… Next… Additionally… Finally… The professor also mentions…

p.217

Weak Response

Evaluation

Score	5	4	3	2	1
Development		V			
Organization		V			
Unity		V			
Language Use	V				

Notes

This essay effectively contrasts the arguments from the reading passage and the lecture. Its organization is also strong with each paragraph explaining the points made in the lecture followed by the contradicting points from the reading. What keeps this response from scoring a 5 is a slight lack of development (especially in the first body paragraph) and occasional lapses in clarity ("It said that missing television causes negative emotions, and this is unlike the reading that said heavy television veiwing creates feelings of loneliness and anxiety"). Overall, this is a solid response held back by a few shortcomings.

Final Score: 4

Critical Analysis

Answer Ⓐ is the correct choice because body paragraph 1 primarily focuses on summarizing the reading passage and includes only one sentence to show contrasting points from the lecture. Body paragraphs 2 and 3 focus primarily on summarizing the lecture, not the reading passage.

Chapter **12** | Independent Writing

Traveling Is Better with a Tour Guide

◈ Generating Ideas
p.218

▷ **Agree**

Reason 1: *Tour guides make all of the arrangements in advance, so you do not have to waste time waiting in lines and so forth. Tour groups also travel in tour buses, which is faster than relying on public transportation.*

Reason 2: *Tour guides are familiar with the area, speak the local language, and know the local customs, so they can more easily deal with problems when they occur.*

Reason 3: *Tour guides know a lot about the places you visit and can explain their history in great detail. You can also easily become friends with the people in your tour group.*

▷ **Disagree**

Reason 1: *By traveling in a tour group, you usually only visit major tourist spots. More adventurous travelers would probably want to visit less popular places.*

Reason 2: *When you are in a tour group, you have fewer opportunities to interact with locals and are rarely placed in new and exciting situations, so the sense of adventure is reduced.*

Reason 3: *Tour groups follow tight schedules, so they visit several different places in a day. As an individual traveler, you can spend more time at places of interest.*

◈ Planning
p.219

Thesis Statement (Agree / Disagree)
I agree with the statement that it is better to travel in a group with a tour guide than to travel alone.

First Supporting Idea
For one, traveling in a group allows you to spend more time enjoying your vacation.

Supporting Example
Tour groups have preplanned itineraries and travel around using tour buses.

Second Supporting Idea
Another benefit of traveling in a tour group is that it makes vacationing safer.

Supporting Example
Tour guides have deep knowledge of the local area, language, and customs, so they can reduce potential risks of traveling.

Conclusion
But for most people, who want to experience the pleasures of a vacation without all of the hassles, traveling in a group with a tour guide is the superior choice.

Strong Response
p.221

Critical Analysis

1 For these reasons, I agree with the statement that it is better to travel in a group with a tour guide than to travel alone. / For one, traveling in a group allows you to spend more time enjoying your vacation. / Another benefit of traveling in a tour group is that it makes

vacationing safer. / But for most people who want to experience the pleasures of a vacation without all of the hassles, traveling in a group with a tour guide is the superior choice.

2 Instead of having to wait in line to buy tickets for every attraction I visited, I was able to enter immediately because the tour guide had already purchased tickets for our tour group. / I also did not have to worry about transportation because my tour group was taken around the city on our own tour bus. / There, I was hiking up a mountain when I tripped on some rocks and broke my ankle. / Had I been alone, without a cell phone, not knowing where to seek medical attention, and not speaking Vietnamese, I might have been in serious trouble. / However, since I was with a tour guide, I was able to get the help I needed quickly and without any problems.

3 tour guides make travel arrangements in advance; do not have to wait in line to buy tickets; do not have to worry about communication problems

have the opportunity to act independently or to learn some of the local customs.

Weak Response   p.223

Evaluation

Score	5	4	3	2	1
Development			V		
Organization			V		
Unity				V	
Language Use			V		

Notes

This response is fairly developed and somewhat well organized. Each paragraph attempts to explain a single idea and includes at least some supporting details. What keeps this essay from scoring higher are the misplaced focus and the abrupt transitions between ideas. The response focuses primarily on the disadvantages of traveling in tour groups without explaining why traveling alone can be better. Furthermore, the transitions between ideas can be abrupt and seemingly random ("my friend want to the vaction also on the tour group. he said they did alot of stuffs and seed many sites. but he could not get relaxed. i thought this way at my vaction. he was so tired after his vaction"). The grammatical problems also obscure the meaning occasionally. For these reasons, this response earns a 3.

Final Score: ___3___

Critical Analysis

Answer Ⓐ is the best choice because body paragraph one argues when you travel with a tour guide, you do not

Part C
Experiencing the TOEFL iBT Actual Tests

≡ Actual Test 01

Task 1 p.227

Listening Script 03-03

Professor: You know, uh, these days, it seems that whenever people get sick, they drop by the pharmacy, pick up some over-the-counter antibiotics, and take them until they get better. Others visit their doctors and ask for prescriptions for more powerful antibiotics. Well, let me tell you something . . . Antibiotics are truly effective; however, you should be cautious when using them. Let me explain why.

First of all, the primary disadvantage of antibiotics is that people are overusing them. That's a problem because many types of bacteria are developing resistance to them. For instance, there is a strain of tuberculosis which has become resistant to multiple antibiotics. TB, as tuberculosis is often known, is a nasty illness that can cause a lot of pain, suffering, and even death. Now, doctors have to find other ways to treat that strain because it's resistant to antibiotics. The same is true of several other bacteria. This will be a huge problem in the future.

I've heard people talk about how antibiotics can help them avoid surgery. That's true, but there's something else you should know. A significant number of people are allergic to antibiotics. Most symptoms are mild, such as red itchy skin and small bumps on the body. Others, such as getting blisters and developing vision problems, are more serious. Some people even go into anaphylactic shock, which can kill them if it's not treated immediately.

Finally, let's keep in mind that some people endure various side effects when they take antibiotics. These can be fevers, headaches, cramps, and diarrhea. In some cases, people get such severe diarrhea that they require hospitalization. Here's another one . . . The antibiotic tetracycline causes photosensitivity in some people. It makes people highly sensitive to light and more susceptible to being sunburned.

Strong Response

The reading passage and the lecture are about antibiotics. In his lecture, the professor casts doubt on the arguments made in the reading passage that antibiotics have numerous benefits.

First, the professor points out that many people are overusing antibiotics. Because people tend to use them whenever they get sick, certain strains of bacteria are developing resistance to antibiotics. He talks about a strain of tuberculosis, which can kill people that cannot be treated by many antibiotics now. In this way, he counters the point made in the reading passage that antibiotics are highly effective.

Next, the professor points out that many people are allergic to antibiotics. He says symptoms may be mild, but they can often be serious and life threatening at times. For instance, after taking antibiotics, some people may suffer from anaphylactic shock, which could kill them. This casts doubt on the argument that antibiotics reduce the need for surgical operations.

Finally, the professor goes against the argument in the reading passage, which claims that antibiotics prevent diseases from spreading and getting worse. He points out that many antibiotics have side effects, including headaches, cramps, and diarrhea, so people taking them can become sicker and need to be hospitalized. Another antibiotic the professor mentions makes people highly sensitive to light, so they can get sunburned easily.

Task 2 p.231

Strong Response

Our lives are defined by the choices we make throughout them. To lead a comfortable and happy life, thorough planning is essential. I therefore agree that in order to have a good future, it is best to plan carefully while you are still young.

The choices you make early in life can have a great impact on your later life. Your actions as a youth create a domino effect that shapes your future, and to lead a good life you must consider the potential consequences. For instance, as a child, I studied languages. Today, I am multilingual. By developing my language skills at an early age, I opened the door for many career opportunities, including translator and international business manager. My brother, on the other hand, neglected his studies when he was young and today has trouble finding jobs that make him happy.

Related to this is the fact that many plans take several years to come to fruition. The careers we have as adults are the results of years or even decades of preparation. Consider the case of my aunt, who is a doctor. In order to become a physician, she had to graduate from medical school. To do that, she had to attend a quality university. To accomplish this, she had to earn good grades during high school. For this to happen, she had to develop proper study habits at a young age.

Finally, creating plans for the future when you are young will allow you to lead a more fulfilling life. People who do not have goals are often unhappy and unsatisfied with their lives. However, you can avoid this by establishing clear goals to work toward at a young age. For instance, when I was in high school, I created the goal of getting straight A's for a semester. When I accomplished this, I derived a great sense of satisfaction, which, in turn, motivated me to work toward my ultimate goal of attending an Ivy League university. Creating short- and long-term goals for myself pushed me to work harder and gave me a sense of purpose in life.

In conclusion, your later life is shaped by the decisions you make when you are young. By planning carefully from a young age, you can ensure that your later life is what you want it to be.

≡ Actual Test 02

Task 1   p.235

Listening   Script 03-07

Professor: Well, class, now let's examine the rise of online news sites and the effect this is having on the way we get our news.

All right, first of all, let's look at the quality of the content on these Internet sites. One of the purported advantages of web-based news sites is their immediate coverage of events. Although news is reported faster online, this is often at the expense of accuracy. What I mean is that in the rush to present the news to readers, sometimes facts are not double-checked. This can result in embarrassingly incorrect stories being published. In fact, it is quite common for online news sites to retract inaccurate information that has already been reported.

In addition, news websites can invade their readers' privacy. While a few sites still let readers browse stories anonymously, an increasing number require readers to submit, you know, personal information before they are given complete access to news articles. This may include giving a full name, an email address, a mailing address, or even the reader's social security number. And what do these sites do with that information? You may think they use it just to customize the news their readers receive, but a lot of times, they also sell this information to advertising companies, which, in turn, contact readers and, um, bombard them with product offers.

And then there is the issue of the global coverage provided by online news sites. For some readers, this

is actually a turnoff. Surveys show that a substantial number of people actually prefer local news coverage because they are, uh, more concerned with what is happening in their community. So rather than reading about things like earthquakes in the Middle East, a lot of people would rather just, uh, read about the events that directly affect them.

Strong Response

The reading passage and the lecture both compare online news websites to traditional printed news. While the reading passage argues in favor of online news sources, the lecturer challenges these claims.

To begin with, the lecturer admits that while news is reported more quickly online, it is done so at the expense of accuracy. Online news articles are not always double-checked, which sometimes leads to embarrassing factual errors. The professor illustrates this by mentioning that news sites sometimes retract inaccurate information that has been published. This contradicts the point made in the reading passage that the immediacy of news websites is always beneficial.

Next, the professor talks about privacy issues. An increasing number of news sites require readers to submit personal information, such as their full name and social security number, before gaining access to news stories. The instructor explains that these news sites often sell readers' personal information to advertising companies. This goes against the reading passage's claim that providing personal information enhances the online news experience.

Finally, the instructor discusses the global news coverage offered by online sites. Some readers are turned off by worldwide coverage and instead prefer local news coverage because they are more interested in reading news about their community. This point rebuts the reading passage's idea that the global news coverage offered by online news sites is strictly an advantage.

Task 2   p.239

Strong Response

Our lives today are almost completely different than the lives of people just two generations ago. Thanks to the Internet and improvements in transportation, I agree that life today is easier and more convenient than when my grandparents were young.

The Internet has made life easier in countless ways. You can shop for virtually anything, stay connected with friends from anywhere in the world, and revisit your favorite childhood television shows all with your computer.

However, the conveniences brought about by the Internet most acutely manifest themselves when looking up information. For example, if my grandfather wanted to learn more about the Civil War, he had to leave his home, go to the local library, search for the books he needed, locate the books on the shelves, and finally locate the information he wanted in the books themselves. The Internet has made all of this much simpler. When I look up information, I simply have to go to the computer, get online, and search for the specific information I want. Thanks to the Internet, I can find the exact information I need within seconds as opposed to the minutes or hours it would have taken in my grandparents' time.

Improvements in transportation have also made our lives easier and more convenient. Today, it is possible to travel virtually anywhere on the globe in less than a day's time, but two generations ago, this was not the case. For instance, consider how my grandfather traveled from Los Angeles to Paris in the 1940s. He took a train to New York, where he boarded a steamship to travel across the Atlantic. Once the boat landed in Europe, he took another train to France. Finally, after traveling for nearly a month, he arrived at his destination. Today, that same trip takes me no more than a day. I simply drive to the Los Angeles airport and, within twelve hours, arrive in Paris all while enjoying the comforts offered by flying. This is just one example of how traveling is much easier and more convenient today than it was sixty years ago.

In summary, I firmly believe that life today is easier and more convenient than it was in my grandparents' time. The Internet has made it possible to learn about anything from the comfort of our homes while advances in travel technology have made it much easier to venture out and explore the world.

TOEFL® MAP
Writing

New TOEFL® Edition

Advanced